GARDEN OF BROKEN STATUES

EXPLORING CENSORSHIP
IN RUSSIA

ACADEMIC
STUDIES
PRESS

GARDEN OF BROKEN STATUES

EXPLORING CENSORSHIP
IN RUSSIA

MARIANNA TAX CHOLDIN

Naomi,
With thanks for
your interest in
this book. I wish
Don could have
seen it!

Boston
2016

Marianna
February 2017

Library of Congress Cataloging-in-Publication Data:
A catalog record for this book is available from
the Library of Congress.

ISBN 978-1-61811-501-0 (hardback)
ISBN 978-1-61811-502-7 (electronic)
ISBN 978-1-61811-544-7 (paperback)

Cover design by Ivan Grave
Photo on the front cover by Harvey Choldin.

Published by Academic Studies Press
28 Montfern Avenue
Brighton, MA 02135, USA
press@academicstudiespress.com
www.academicstudiespress.com

To the memory of Katia Genieva

CONTENTS

INTRODUCTION

I was sitting with Katia Genieva, my Russian partner and close friend, in velvet-covered seats in the ornate theater of the Palace of Congresses in the Moscow Kremlin. It was October 1992, and I'd just arrived for one of my weeklong stays to work with Katia on the censorship exhibition we were to open in her library, the Library for Foreign Literature, the following May. It was early evening, dark and snowy in this northern city. I was jet-lagged—there was a nine-hour time change working against me—and my eyes felt gritty; I hoped I'd be able to stay awake. It was uncomfortably warm in the hall, but what agitated me most was the intense awareness of being in the Kremlin, the center of Soviet power. I remembered this feeling from earlier visits in Soviet times, a kind of uneasy claustrophobia. Stalin's ghost is everywhere.

This evening we were in the Palace of Congresses not to see *Swan Lake* or a folk ensemble, nor for any kind of political function, but to see and hear a Christian rock group perform. And perform they did, with great energy and verve, to the joy of the packed house. I managed somehow to stay awake, aided by drums and electric guitars at high volume. At intermission, the ushers, older women dressed in black, glared disapprovingly at the mostly youthful audience, dressed in Western jeans and sweatshirts—certainly not appropriate attire for this grand Soviet palace of culture.

In my woozy state, I wondered whether this could really be happening. Was I perhaps dreaming? *A religious rock concert in the Kremlin?* I pinched myself. No, it wasn't a dream. The music blared, the musicians gyrated, the audience screamed approvingly. Religion and rock music had been forbidden topics under Communism, no doubt about that. And here I was, with all these people around me swaying and bobbing their heads and screaming in their velvet seats, being bombarded by these sights and sounds *in the Kremlin*, the heart of the empire! Amazing. Yes, the Soviet Union must truly have disappeared.

I'd seen it coming over the past few years, even while the Soviet Union still existed. One bright spring day, my Russian friend Galia Levina and I had taken some visiting Americans on a small cruise on the Moscow River. Our fellow passengers were ordinary people: a grandma with her small granddaughter, a pair of lovers, some tourists from other parts of the Soviet Union enjoying the lovely weather. In a low, conversational voice, Galia had begun to tell me about her grandfather, a scientist, and how he suffered under Stalin. The grandmother sitting near us leaned over and chimed in with a story about her father, who had been taken away in 1938 and resurfaced in 1957. Other passengers nodded and offered their own family stories. Suddenly, strangers on a boat were sharing intimate tales of horror, all drawn together in a net of memory. Their voices grew louder as they shook their heads and poured out their tales to each other. Speechless, I peered in from outside.

Before that day, I had never experienced anything remotely like this in the Soviet Union. People simply didn't talk about such things in a public place, among strangers. You might be seen as anti-Soviet, and you didn't know who might be listening. No, better to lock up your pain in your heart.

Life was full of such surprises in the years leading up to December 31, 1991, when the Soviet Union collapsed. You could arrive at your hotel from the airport, walk into your room, turn on your TV, and find yourself staring in disbelief at none other than Leon Trotsky on the screen. Trotsky was well known in the West as the Communist leader who didn't make it to the top and had to take refuge in Mexico, where Soviet agents eventually murdered him. His very name couldn't be printed or uttered during Stalin's reign, and if you broke the rules, you might well be sent to the gulag or shot. Now here he was on television, portrayed by a respectable Soviet actor, in a play about revolutionary times aimed at a wide audience. I sank into a chair, seriously disoriented. Where was I?

One day, when post-Soviet Russia was less than a year old, Katia sent me to the Russian State Library, formerly the Lenin State Library, known in

Soviet times and now as the Leninka, or Dear Little Lenin Library (Russians love to give their beloved buildings ironic nicknames). I was there for the opening ceremony of an exhibition of Russian Orthodox publications, treasures of the library's collection. Most people had no idea these books were there because they had been locked up in what was arguably the world's largest *spetskhran*, or special closed collection, an institution of great importance in the Soviet system. The Leninka's *spetskhran* held millions of items—books, magazines, newspapers, pamphlets, and other objects that had been, for a variety of reasons, banned during Soviet times. Among them were, of course, thousands of books dealing with religion, including Russian Orthodoxy and other world religions.

People who lived in the Soviet Union knew that religious books were never accessible to ordinary people. Religion was the opiate of the masses (*"das Opium des Volkes,"* in Marx's words), and religious books were deemed dangerous. But that day in the Leninka, they were being exhibited and celebrated. And who was on the stage, along with the Leninka's director and Aleksandr Rutskoi, then vice president of Russia and quite a high-ranking politician to grace the stage at an exhibition? None other than the patriarch of all Russia and spiritual head of the Russian Orthodox Church, Aleksy II, with his impressive gray beard, priestly black robes, decorative white headdress, and large gold cross on his breast. The patriarch was there to bless the exhibit opening.

For the first time in decades of Russian and Soviet history, the significance of an entire category of books was being tacitly acknowledged, but with no explanation or opportunity for discussion. Suddenly, religion was not only acceptable but also highly honored, presented with pomp and showered with blessings. I took pictures to convince myself later that this really had happened. The patriarch, in ceremonial regalia, really did appear before the television cameras in a packed hall in the Lenin Library, that temple of atheism. He really did bless us, along with those Orthodox books that had been hidden from the public for decades, the mere mention of which had sent thousands of priests, scholars, and believers to the gulag.

These incidents and many more like them made me dizzy, as though I'd been pushed off-balance. They came hard and fast, and I didn't have time to analyze them, to understand what, beyond the superficial shock, struck me so deeply. I made notes and put off analysis until sometime later.

The beginning of an answer came on a dreary November day in 1997. Harvey, my husband, and I, along with an American and a Russian friend, were strolling in a park in central Moscow near the new building of the Tretyakov Gallery. As I looked around that park, I realized I had stumbled into a place that was going to be important for me. I asked Harvey to take a few pictures so I could look at them later and sort out my thoughts.

GARDEN OF BROKEN STATUES TOUR, STOP 1: INTRODUCTION TO THE GARDEN

Clearly, we were in no ordinary park, with flowers and benches and children's play equipment. This park was a place where Soviet-era sculptures had been gathered together, uprooted from their pedestals around the city and then abandoned. Among trees, bare and black on this cold, rainy November day, they stood, some nobly upright, others dumped ignominiously on their sides—or perhaps they had started out upright and fallen over or been pushed. There were Lenin and Stalin, of course, and Felix Dzerzhinsky, founder of the Soviet secret police, nicknamed "Iron Felix" and "Bloody Felix," and many more unnamed, unfamiliar figures.

Two Socialist-Realist statues being moved into the Garden of Broken Statues
(November 1997)

I called this park the Garden of Broken Statues, and the images of those statues lodged in the back of my mind, together with the other images I saw and accumulated in my notes and my memory in the course of the 1990s and early 2000s.

I was too busy absorbing all the changes taking place in Russia to sort it all out then, as I had promised myself to do, and more than fifteen years passed before I was able to think clearly about the garden. As I organized my thoughts to write this book, I found myself returning again and again to some of the statues and monuments and museums I had seen in the former Soviet Union and its neighbors during these early post-Soviet years, and I imagined a kind of garden tour that linked them to one another. A stop on the tour looks like this:

Statue of Lenin in the garden

Statue of Stalin in the garden

Foreground: Leonid Brezhnev, general secretary of the Central Committee of
the Communist Party of the Soviet Union, 1964–1982, presider over the
"Era of Stagnation." Background: "The Soviet Union, Stronghold of Peace"
(Garden of Broken Statues)

GARDEN OF BROKEN STATUES TOUR, STOP 2:
KGB CONFERENCE

In October 1993, on our way to the airport for my flight home, Katia decided to stop for half an hour at a conference in progress, "The KGB, Yesterday, Today, and Tomorrow."

I shook myself when I saw the title, which suggested to me any number of conferences being held in hotels in the United States: "Good Nutrition Yesterday, Today, and Tomorrow" or "Redeveloping Neighborhood Design Yesterday, Today, and Tomorrow." But the KGB? The very name struck fear into my heart, and I was not even a victim of this secret police force with its unspeakably bloody history, this institution that had terrorized and abused the Soviet people for so long.

The session featured KGB agents onstage, beautifully dressed in suits and being yelled at by scruffy former dissidents and gulag survivors in worn leather jackets. I left for the airport feeling shaken by the anger in that room but amused and gratified by the scene: the dreaded KGB men looked pretty silly in their elegant clothes, not scary at all as they mouthed lame excuses for their collective unspeakable behavior. The KGB had transformed even its appearance, exchanging badly made Soviet clothes for suits of a fine cut. (On his first trip to Leningrad, in 1978, Harvey looked around him at the sea of Soviet jeans and dark overcoats that didn't hang right and murmured, "So this is the price they paid for getting rid of all the Jewish tailors!")

I revisit that KGB conference in my memory from time to time. How deep are the changes? I caution myself to question this institution's new image, not to accept it at face value. There is probably more going on here than meets the eye. After all, the KGB is part of the new Russia. What role will it play?

GARDEN OF BROKEN STATUES TOUR, STOP 3:
VILNIUS, LITHUANIA, KGB MUSEUM

In July 1998, I visited an unforgettable site in Vilnius, the capital of formerly Soviet Lithuania. Guides who had been inmates took some colleagues and me through a particularly grisly museum in the building

"The KGB, Yesterday, Today, and Tomorrow" (Moscow, February 1993)

that had housed the KGB prison during Soviet times. As Lithuania was becoming independent, local Soviet authorities attempted to cover up the execution chamber, but zealous Lithuanians refused to let this happen. Thanks to recent work by archeologists, I could see beneath the hastily erected false floor the real floor stained with prisoners' blood as they were shot. I can't recall specifics because as soon as I realized where I was, I couldn't bear it, and I squeezed my eyes shut. I took no photographs.

CHAPTER 1

MY AMERICAN PLANET

North America is my home planet and Chicago my anchor city, but Hyde Park is the South Side neighborhood where I was born in 1942 and grew up and was the epicenter of my first twenty years. In Hyde Park we lived five minutes' walk from the University of Chicago campus, where Papa taught anthropology. We were close to Lake Michigan to the east and not far from the Stockyards to the west. The poet Carl Sandburg called Chicago "Hog Butcher for the World," and sometimes, when the wind was just right, the fishy smell from the lake and the stink of freshly killed meat from the slaughterhouses would meet over the six-flat apartment building where I spent my first eleven years and the house one block to the east where I lived until I graduated from college and married Harvey. There was soot in the air from the steel mills a few miles south along the lake—our white curtains turned black so quickly that Mama and Grandma were always washing them. At night, the flames from the mills' chimneys lit up the sky. We could hear the Illinois Central Railroad trains roll by on their tracks a few blocks toward the lake; I often fell asleep to the gentle rhythm of the wheels.

My earliest memories are of that apartment on University Avenue. The campus was my playground, and many of the world-famous professors were just the parents of my friends, as far as I was concerned. One of my best friends in my early years at the university's Laboratory Schools was Barbara, stepdaughter of Robert Maynard Hutchins, chancellor of the university (later president) and a giant among intellectuals throughout the country. Still today people speak of Hutchins with awe, but to me he was just Barbara's father.

Sol Tax (1979) (University of Chicago Photographic Archive, apf1-08217,
Special Collections Research Center, University of Chicago Library)

Barbara lived in the president's house a couple of blocks down the street, but we practically lived in each other's houses. She was the only child in the house at that time, and her parents welcomed her friendship with me, including me in private French lessons and on weekend trips to their country place on a little island in a lake northwest of the city. Mr. Hutchins had a driver who picked us up in a nice black car, and we spent the hour and a half riding to the island happily engrossed in conversation. Barbara's father never talked down to me; he asked me what I thought of this and that, and I responded and asked questions of my own. What was I reading these days? *The Red Book of Fairy Tales?* What were some of my favorites? And we'd talk about fairy tales for a while. Then I'd ask him what he was reading, and he'd tell me—a book about philosophy—and ask whether it sounded interesting to me. Yes, I'd answer honestly, because he explained so clearly what the book was about, and the time would fly by. On the island we spent hours in a rowboat; Mr. Hutchins loved to fish, and neither Barbara nor her mother shared his passion. I had never fished before and felt queasy when he baited his hook and even more so when he caught a fish. I tangled my line hopelessly, and he patiently untangled it as we sat in the boat and talked for hours.

I didn't realize it then, but growing up with people in high places—our apartment building housed at various times three Nobel Prize laureates and hosted as visitors a number of domestic and foreign dignitaries—put me completely at ease with figures of authority. The house we moved into later was home to Enrico Fermi during the Manhattan Project, when the first atomic bomb was developed. I wondered how Fermi's kids had liked it. Later in life, when I encountered people in academic or political life who inspired awe or fear in my friends and colleagues, I would think to myself, "Oh, well, he's just some kid's father."

I was a very early reader and benefited from my sister, Susan, nearly four years older. As long as I can remember, books have been an important part of my life. My school, which was part of the university, had two excellent libraries. The librarians and the collections in both were outstanding, and I read whatever I wanted. In the summers I rode my bicycle to the nearby branch of the Chicago Public Library, where I wandered through the entire collection, filled up my bicycle basket with books, and pedaled home. No one told me what I should or should not read, and as a child I assumed that this was true everywhere.

I don't know when I first heard or read the term "censorship," but by the time I did, I was already vigorously opposed to it. I suppose I picked up that attitude from my parents and the milieu in which I lived, because even as a kid I believed I should be able to read anything I wanted and thought all children were capable of doing the same. I had no interest in *Reader's Digest* abridged books or young peoples' editions of classics: I wanted to make up my own mind and form my own opinions. My parents, teachers, and librarians encouraged me in this view, and both at home and at school I was treated as an adult when it came to reading.

In addition to my strong convictions about the freedom to read, I also possessed a love of great ideas eloquently expressed. I knew that our Constitution, the basis of our government, included something called the First Amendment that guaranteed freedom of speech and freedom of the press to all citizens. I felt so strongly about the subject that I even memorized a phrase written by one of my American heroes, Thomas Jefferson: "I have sworn upon the altar of God eternal hostility against every form of tyranny over the mind of man." A few years later, while studying German, I learned the rousing song "*Die Gedanken sind frei*": "thoughts are free, no one can catch them."

My fascination with these strong ideals—some carved in marble, others expressed in poetry or music—is the basis for my lifelong interest in monuments and the stories they tell. Over the decades I've wandered through countless cemeteries in many countries, poring over elaborate inscriptions on the mausoleums of rich and powerful people as well as weed-covered nameless graves. I got my start close to home, at Oak Woods Cemetery, Chicago's oldest, where my family's plots reside, and as a child I was drawn to the "Confederate Mound," where some six thousand Confederate prisoners of war are buried.

But it wasn't only graves that spoke to me as a child; all monuments intrigued me. I grew up among Chicago's many statues commemorating heroes, often mounted grandly on horses. I've always been especially moved by little-known monuments that people often miss. One that comes to mind is Fort Dearborn, established thirty-four years before the city itself and destroyed by the widening of the Chicago River and Great Fire of 1871. Its corners are marked by metal strips on either side of the river, which runs through downtown, and when I was little, I used to stop and stare intently at those last remnants, imagining the fort in all its glory. Only later did I learn that not all monuments are glorious, that they may commemorate villains as well as heroes, and that their messages may be lies masquerading as truth.

I don't know when I first heard the word "tolerance" either, but I embraced the concept around the same time I learned to talk. "Some people are different than other people!" I remember marching through the halls of our apartment building at the age of three or four, announcing this truth to our neighbors, much to the consternation of my grammatically correct mother.

"Different *from* other people, Nana," she would instruct me. "Different from, not different than." (As a little girl, I couldn't pronounce "Marianna" and called myself "Nana"; the name stuck, and I was Nana to the family for many years. Now I am Nana again, to my granddaughters!) Friends and family laughed indulgently, and I look back on my toddler self and laugh, too, and with great affection at the memory of my distraught mother, who never could tolerate even minor grammatical errors.

Today I realize that my "difference mantra" still lies deep inside me, as does my dislike of censorship and my fascination with monuments, and that these three characteristics—tolerance for people different from myself, the rejection of controls on thought and expression, and my intense interest in a community's history as expressed through tangible symbols—were woven into the fabric of my being in early childhood and grew into the passions that color the cloth of my adult being.

My parents always accepted differences among people as something quite natural. For Papa, the anthropologist, something we in the family perceived as *different* was to be observed, described, discussed. It might strike us as positive or negative, but it was always interesting and worthy of attention and respect. He gently admonished me whenever I declared something (liver, stewed tomatoes) bad. "Let's just say, 'I don't like it,'" he would urge.

In the 1940s and 1950s, we lived in a liberal bubble surrounded by eminent scholars from all over the world. My family and our circle of friends believed strongly in critical thinking, tolerance of differences, and freedom of expression. Not everyone in Hyde Park was a liberal, of course; we, too, had our far-righties and far-lefties, which made for animated discussions. But this bubble, my cocoon, provided me with a warm, peaceful, safe childhood environment within the university community. There is some irony, I suppose, in the fact that a great university filled with brilliant, feisty, and argumentative thinkers exploring every aspect of life should be perceived as a warm, peaceful, safe place. After all, a few weeks before my birth, scientists from all over the world initiated the first artificial, self-sustaining, nuclear chain reaction in an artificial nuclear reactor just a few blocks from our apartment and the ice rink where I skated on weekend mornings. Some cocoon! And yet that's what Hyde Park was for me.

I began to emerge from the cocoon when I was seven or eight and started to hear about Senator Joseph McCarthy and the word "McCarthyism."

My parents and their friends were always talking about the senator from Wisconsin, and they must have explained their concerns to me, because I was certainly aware that people in our circle were upset and angry, and I was too.

When I was ten or eleven, I found myself for the first time in the middle of a real-life freedom-of-expression issue. A close school friend confided that she wanted to buy some books by Marx and Engels. Her parents were quite conservative, so instead of having the books mailed to her house, she asked whether my parents would receive them. They easily agreed, reasoning that my friend's parents were sending her to a school where she was exposed to a wide range of ideas in the liberal community of Hyde Park and that they wouldn't object to her reading such material in that context. Afterward, for some time we were regular recipients of "dangerous books" such as *The Communist Manifesto*. I wasn't interested in Marx and Engels in those days, but I thought it important that no one prevent us from reading such books if we wanted to.

In 1954 when I was twelve, the country began coming to its senses in its rejection of McCarthyism. I vividly remember watching special television coverage of the US Senate McCarthy hearings with my family on our very first television set. Now I really understood, to my horror, that right there in my own lifetime my country had not been such a wonderful and free place, despite our glorious Constitution and First Amendment.

Not that I was ever attracted to Communism—far from it. As a child I was pretty negative about Communism, largely because of an incident from Papa's past that he'd told us about more than once. He was quite firmly anti-Communist, having been burned while an undergraduate at the University of Wisconsin in the 1920s. Communists had taken over the Young Liberals Club, which he chaired, and he abhorred the methods they'd used. His description of the takeover was vivid, and I've never forgotten it. When I became interested in Russia, he and I talked about the Bolshevik takeover of the Russian Provisional Government in October 1917, and an image of that takeover meeting at the Young Liberals Club attached itself to my image of the Bolsheviks' takeover.

As a small child I was drawn to archaeology. When I was five or six, Papa brought home an orangutan skull from the office because he had a hunch I'd be interested. I loved that skull and wanted to take it to school for show-and-tell, so he helped me prepare a little talk for my classmates. I was dismayed when several of them shrieked and made disgusting noises when I held up the skull, and the teacher had to intervene. She and I were the only people who gave that skull the respectful attention it deserved, and I've always been sorry that I didn't get to deliver my speech to anyone but Miss Thurston. Another time, one of my classmates said something belittling about Australian Aborigines or Pygmies. I reared up with a severe little speech about how these indigenous people had a highly developed social organization, and I became something of an anthropological pest at school.

When I was seven or eight, however, a toy nurse's kit turned me on to medicine, and I told my parents I wanted to be a nurse.

"How about a doctor instead?" Papa asked. He arranged for me to observe an operation on a rabbit at the university hospital and bought me a copy of *Gray's Anatomy*. But maybe that slab-sized *Gray's Anatomy* was too much and drove me out of medicine; soon I was back into archaeology. I was eleven in 1953, when Papa brought home news of a great anthropological hoax that had just been revealed: Piltdown Man, supposedly an important link in the evolutionary chain, turned out to be no link at all but rather a fake, cleverly assembled by one Charles Dawson. I was terrifically intrigued, and with Papa's encouragement I wrote a "novel" about it (many pages in a small notebook or two but, alas, only seventeen pages typed). Intellectual honesty, I realized, was a very important quality.

Archaeology seemed exotic to me, but cultural anthropology I took for granted: it was part of everyday life. Our home was filled with objects that had been part of the family households in Panajachel, where Papa, Mama, and Susan lived before I was born, and Mexico City, where I spent the first year of my life. I grew up with stories of the annual trips on United Fruit Company banana boats to Guatemala, where Mama was introduced to what became our favorite dessert, sliced bananas in orange juice. A prosaic dessert, to be sure, but offered up on a banana boat carrying my family to Guatemala, it struck me as exotic and elegant. Served in a shallow glass bowl, it remains a Proustian memory. I was too young to remember the earthquake caused by the birth of the volcano named Paricutin that shook Mexico City a few days before my first birthday, but I've heard the story many times of how Antonia, our maid, pulled Susan and me under the threshold of the door for safety. (Mama and Papa were across the city in a cinema, watching *Gone with the Wind*!) I've heard, too, that I cried bitterly at my birthday party when Susan and other older children smashed a piñata that showered candy around me. Mama used to tell me that when she pushed me in my buggy along the Paseo de la Reforma, Mexico City's grand avenue, people would stop to admire me, telling Mama that I was a pretty baby "even though I had dark hair—a pity I wasn't blonde."

Throughout my childhood, Mama, Papa, and Susan spoke Spanish and English interchangeably, while Mama and Papa spoke Yiddish with Mama's mother, who lived with us. I absorbed both languages and French too, from my lessons with Barbara Hutchins, although I never spoke fluently. Yiddish I identified with Grandma and French with Barbara, but Spanish represented a larger world. Friends from Mexico and Guatemala came frequently to visit, and we played with dozens of tiny children's toys, mainly from Guatemala and collected in a curio cabinet from Papa's boyhood home in

Mama, Papa, Susan, Marianna (in Papa's arms) (Mexico City 1942)

Milwaukee. (My daughters and niece played with the collection, and Harvey's and my granddaughters enjoy it today, enhanced by a few later additions from Russia.)

Life with an anthropologist was exciting. We helped Papa collate the galley pages of his book about the highlands of Guatemala, *Penny Capitalism*, on the living room floor of our apartment. We took working vacations each summer and several times drove to Tama, Iowa, to the Mesquaki/Fox Indian reservation, where Papa developed his theory of action anthropology. I remember clearly how Susan, Mama, and I danced with the women and children during powwows. Once we traveled to Fort Berthold, North Dakota, an Indian reservation that was home to several American Indian tribes. I remember being blissfully happy to be living in a big silver trailer and playing with local kids on the reservation while Papa consulted with grown-ups about Garrison Dam, soon to flood them out.

We took many family car trips, working vacations for Papa and pure vacation for Mama, Susan, and me. (Grandma usually went to stay with her sons in Detroit, Uncle Mike and Uncle George, while we were gone.) One trip in the late 1940s or early 1950s left a deep impression on me. We had driven to Talladega College in Alabama, a historically black school where Papa had been invited to lecture. I saw plenty of poverty on that trip, but what really horrified me was my first experience of segregation. When we stopped at a gas station with separate bathrooms and drinking fountains for "Negroes," I felt as if someone had punched me in the stomach. I went to school with Negroes; there were Negro professors at the University of Chicago whom my parents revered; we had Negro friends in the neighborhood. The woman who cleaned for us was Negro, and so was the postman, whom Mama called "Mr." and whom we all treated with respect. I knew about segregation; we talked about it at school and at home—but I wasn't prepared to encounter it at the gas station, and it really hurt.

Certainly the car trip that I remember most clearly was in the summer of 1950, when we drove to Berkeley, where Papa taught for the summer. That trip—along US highways for much of the time, no interstate highways yet—was tortuous and at the same time delightful. Parents in the front seat, smoking, with the windows rolled up to prevent drafts. Children in the back seat, not always happily. I would have loved to read, but it made me carsick, so much of the time I dozed, listening to the Weavers singing "Good Night, Irene" on the radio and dreaming of Joe DiMaggio, our current hero. Sometimes we squabbled in the back seat; Papa wrecked our maroon Chevy in Colby, Kansas, driving off a little bridge into a dry river bed, probably at least partly because of a disagreement between Susan and me over who had encroached on whose backseat turf. (He liked driving, but I don't think he was awfully good at it, and no doubt the squawking behind him caused a distraction.) We spent the night in Colby while the car was being repaired. My travels haven't taken me there since, but I'll never forget that little town. I can still see the gas station where our poor, damaged Chevy lay and feel the intense heat of a Kansas summer enveloping me.

We spent the whole summer of 1952 in New York City, where Papa did some work with the Wenner-Gren Foundation for Anthropological Research. We lived in a huge apartment on Central Park West that holds a special place in my memory because it belonged to a concert pianist and had two Steinway concert grands in the palatial living room. Susan and I fed the squirrels in Central Park and swam at the YWCA. That was a lovely summer.

In 1957 Papa, Susan, and I flew to Mexico City for three weeks, my first flight and my first time out of the United States since my trip to Mexico at the age of four months. The airline was Air France, and the food and service were elegant. The night we arrived, we visited an acquaintance, a wealthy and cultured German expat who lived in a large and beautiful apartment. I recall a sumptuous dinner and probably had a sip of wine, feeling very worldly and sophisticated. After we ate, our host showed us some of his treasures, and while standing in front of a framed letter from Mozart to someone, I fainted. (Was Mozart to blame?) I was so embarrassed! Papa and our host both assured me that I just wasn't used to Mexico City's seven-thousand-foot elevation and that it wasn't uncommon to faint on the first day. But I was fifteen years old and humiliated, and nothing they said made me feel any better.

In Mexico City, however, I was introduced to a kind of poverty I'd never seen before; the contrast between rich and poor stunned me. After some days we flew south to Oaxaca in a small plane, making what seemed to me to be an impossible landing between mountains—quite a shock after Air France—and I saw for the first time how peasants lived, in villages with small cottages

Marianna, Papa, Susan (Chiapas, Mexico, 1957) (University of Chicago
Photographic Archive, apf1-08197, Special Collections Research Center,
University of Chicago Library)

without electricity or indoor plumbing. I had no idea how old the adults
actually were because many were toothless, and some of the children looked
malnourished. Still, they struck me as better off than the urban poor I'd seen,
because their living conditions weren't as crowded and dirty. And the lines
between these peasants, largely Mayan Indians, and the non-Indians, mostly
of Spanish descent and higher on the social scale, seemed blurrier than our
very definite black and white lines at home.

We were driven through the mountains, and those trips made a deep
and terrifying impression on me, maybe even more than the landing between

two mountains. I was sure that our driver, Lauro, drove too fast—my stomach told me so—but he took the hairpin curves skillfully. I tried closing my eyes, but that brought me to the edge of nausea, so I looked out the window. As we rushed past the curves, I couldn't help but see large white crosses, indicating the spot when a car or bus had gone over, driven by a less skillful driver. I looked at Lauro's hands on the steering wheel, relaxed and confident, and I developed something of a crush on him, mixed with the giddiness of relief that we were safe.

We grew up with so many stories about Mama and Papa and their families and their lives before we were born. Mama talked lovingly about New Glarus, the village in Wisconsin where she grew up after Grandpa and Grandma Katz left New York City. The citizens of New Glarus, all eight hundred of them, were descendants of immigrants from the Swiss canton of Glarus who left during the European revolutions of 1848. They still spoke the Swiss-German of their ancestors and understood Mama's family's Yiddish without difficulty. We heard about Mama's friends, her school, her house with the big garden that she and Grandma tended, the chickens they raised, the farms and cheese factory that supported the village. She told us about Grandpa's tragic death: he collected scrap metal, and one day the brakes failed on his truck while he was standing behind it and he was run over. Mama was only eighteen.

Papa's stories were not bucolic at all. He was a city boy who lived in Milwaukee with his parents, two brothers, and a big sister, with a large extended family nearby. Two of my favorite stories are from his college and graduate student years: his trip to Algeria with a Beloit College expedition, from which he brought back a marvelous Bedouin shawl, a piece of sandstone we called "the rose of the Sahara," a photo of himself in Bedouin dress, and a wonderful account of the Passover seders he enjoyed with two Algerian families and his first field season, with famous anthropologist Ruth Benedict in New Mexico in 1931, when he hitchhiked home, lost his suitcase with all his field notes in it to a dishonest driver, and was picked up by the driver of a fancy car whose wife somehow sensed Papa's resemblance to a rabbi who had "cured" their baby and turned out to be Papa's grandfather!

Susan graduated from the University of Chicago Laboratory School in 1954, and Papa gave the commencement address, "The Freedom to Make

Grandma Katz (May 24, 1953)

Mistakes." It was a bold and elegant talk, advocating rights for children and everyone else, and I love rereading it, because it always reminds me of the way Papa handled me when I decided to try smoking. I was five or six, I think. Both parents smoked a pack a day at that time (they stopped later), and I wanted to know what smoking was all about. I sneaked a pack (Camels? Lucky Strikes?) and a book of matches out of Mama's purse and went somewhere nearby to light up. I knew that what I was doing was dangerous, but that didn't stop me.

Of course, Mama noticed immediately and said that Papa would deal with me. Then there was nothing for it but to run away from home. I didn't want to, as I loved our apartment and my family, but as I saw it, I had disgraced myself and had to leave. (I wasn't afraid of physical punishment; that wasn't done in our family.) I trudged down University Avenue, where we lived at the time, with my favorite doll. Papa came after me, and we walked together for a while, in silence. Then he said, "I understand you'd like to try smoking, and I think you should. Let's go home and smoke together." We turned around, walked back to our apartment building, and sat on the front steps. He lit two cigarettes and gave me one, instructing me how to hold it and how to inhale. I did, and of course, I choked and coughed. All the while he talked to me quietly, explaining why I might want to give up smoking before I got started. I didn't argue.

We had another of our walk-and-talk sessions a few years later, when I was ten or eleven. I had developed an intense fear of death, which woke me up at night and kept me in a state of terror. My fear was so huge that I didn't want to talk about it: too scary. But Papa coaxed it out of me one day as we were walking home from school. He listened intently, then began talking to me about girls my age. Our bodies were changing, he explained, and maybe my intense feelings, common to girls in other cultures too, were related to the changes occurring in my body. I was so relieved to know that I wasn't alone, that other girls might be worried too. We didn't resolve the question of death, of course, but he certainly did make me feel better; my terror subsided, and I slept well again.

I embarked on perhaps my greatest Papa-inspired adventure in the fall of 1959, when he sprang the idea of translating an anthropological treatise. He caught me at a good time: I was in my last year of high school, in Herr Heggen's third-year German class, confident about my German-language ability after two summers living with families in Germany. I guess it's unusual, to say the least, for a seventeen-year-old to translate a scholarly treatise from German into English and see it published by a prominent publishing house (the University of Chicago Press) by the time she's twenty-one and in her third year of college. My accomplishment would have paled 150 years earlier next to the everyday achievements of one of my heroes, John Stuart Mill, who was translating from Greek and Latin at the age of four! I'm certainly no Mill, but I loved languages and was good at learning them, and in doing this work I developed a deep moral commitment to producing a translation that reflected the author's intent.

Certainly I would never have attempted the book project, or even thought of it, on my own, but Papa had perfect confidence in his daughters and was always urging us on to follow adventurous paths. When he suggested that I translate Adolf Jensen's *Mythos und Kult bei Naturvölkern* (Myth and Cult among Primitive Peoples) into English, I recall arguing with him.

"Papa," I said, "I'm just a kid! My German is pretty good, but I'm not an anthropologist. I wouldn't know how to begin!"

"Begin at the beginning," he advised me. "Sit down at the typewriter and translate the first couple of paragraphs of the introduction. I'll show them to the author and, if he likes them, to someone at the press, and then we'll see."

So I did, and to my great amazement the author, and subsequently the press, judged my first attempt satisfactory. In Papa's papers, housed in the University of Chicago Archives, is a letter to him in German from Professor Jensen dated January 7, 1960, in which he thanks Professor Dr. Tax for his letter of December 21, 1959. He writes: "I learned with great interest that Miss or Mrs. M.T. would like to do the translation. Based on the sample that was sent, I consider her to be thoroughly suitable." I went to the press with Papa and agreed to produce a draft of the book in the next eighteen months. Wolfgang Weissleder, a doctoral student in the Department of Anthropology whose native language was German, would revise it, and the press would publish it.

I understand now that the path was not entirely smooth: based on a reader's report, the editors had some reservations about my translation, which was very literal; although it was what they asked me to produce, I imagine it looked rough. A memo to Papa from Carroll Bowen, assistant director of the press, dated January 17, 1961, says: "It seems clear from the attached reader's report that the translation needs careful attention still. What would you suggest?"

Papa wrote a note by hand on the memo: "She will eventually get you a 1st rate MS; she has her copy from Jensen returned to her with some comments but many compliments. It will do her good to know that her German is sometimes not perfect. Send on the comment—but directly to her not to me (though I'll carry the MS home to her)."

The editors knew Papa well; he was actively involved with the press for many years and was at one time chairman of the Press Board. His status certainly assured me an audition, so to speak, but I don't believe the press was pressured into accepting me as translator. I was conscientious and hardworking, applied myself wholeheartedly to the German text, and wrote English well. Weissleder's task was to turn my English into "anthropologese." Together, we produced a translation published by the press, in hardcover and paperback, in 1963.

Hyde Park, my school, my friends' homes, and frequent trips to downtown Chicago constituted my larger world, but our University Avenue apartment and, later, the house on Woodlawn Avenue were intimate places where I spent the first twenty years of my life. Probing my memory, I've discovered another lens through which I saw the world as a small child—a Jewish lens—and through it I became aware for the first time of Russia. My grandparents on both my parents' sides had emigrated from the Russian Empire at the beginning of the twentieth century, when pogroms were rampant. Like so many, my grandparents came to the United States to make a better life for themselves, their children, and their grandchildren.

Papa's people came from around Zhitomir, near Kiev, and from other Jewish shtetls in the Pale of Settlement. I never knew his parents; heart attacks felled them both as relatively young people. The grandma who lived with us was Mama's mother. Grandma Katz had grown up in the Pale and spent her married life in Uzda, a town not far from Minsk in what is now Belarus, near Vilna (the Yiddish name for Vilnius), the capital of present-day Lithuania.

The Russian language lay buried deep in Grandma's memory, covered over by a thick layer of Yiddish, the language she spoke and read fluently, and by very spotty English. She talked with the family in Yiddish, which my parents spoke adequately, and while my sister and I understood her, we responded mainly in English. We both studied German in school and mixed it with our rudimentary Yiddish when we spoke with Grandma.

When Susan and I were little, Grandma used to tell us stories, always in Yiddish, the same ones she had told my mother when she was growing up: folk tales that I recognized later as Russian but with Jewish overtones, full of snow and wolves chasing small children. She shared vivid recollections of her life in what is now Ukraine and Belarus. I remember especially her story about the Cossacks riding through town when she was a young girl, perhaps my age or younger, and how her mother made her stay hidden indoors. We never talked about what might have happened had the Cossacks seen her; I knew by her expression, her voice, her gestures that it was too terrible to put into words. Certainly Grandma had nothing good to say about Russia, past or present. She despised and feared Stalin, even from the safe distance of Hyde Park. Yet I was drawn to that motherland that had rejected my people, pushed us out.

Grandma told us how, due to some bureaucratic mix-up, she had to spend a night in jail at the border as she left Russia to take a ship to join her husband in New York. (This happened in 1900 or so.) We have a photograph of Grandma's father, a rabbi who was highly respected, she told us; he was buried in the highest part of the cemetery, which was reserved for honored members of the community. We also have some letters from towns in what is now Belarus and Lithuania, where family members lived. Letters moved slowly, uncertainly. World War I happened and the Bolshevik revolution, and there was still some contact by mail. But in those days, when you emigrated, you left for good. You never saw your loved ones again.

Correspondence ended abruptly during World War II, and when Grandma tried to resume it after the war, her letters were returned marked "no such place." This war was different. A few of my family's relatives and friends had come to America or to Palestine around the same time Grandma and Grandpa did: Grandpa's brother and sister, several of my grandmother's siblings too. And on my father's side, the same story. They, the lucky ones, escaped the second war. The rest? Where they lived, mostly in war zones, I imagine they were not so fortunate. Many, perhaps most, were exterminated on the spot and buried in mass graves, black Soviet soil shoveled over them. I never knew their names, but they haunt me, my lost Jewish family. I say Kaddish for them.

I watched Grandma as she kept up with events in the Soviet Union through her cover-to-cover reading of *The Daily Forward*, the Yiddish newspaper published in New York. She would often read aloud, in a low voice that became fierce and angry when she came across Stalin's name, and she would tell my mother what a bad man he was. I didn't detect any of my Russia-love in Grandma.

Grandma was around ninety when I began college. Once, when I was just beginning to learn Russian, she heard me practicing some sentences out loud and spontaneously began responding to me in what I realized must be her second native tongue, along with Yiddish.

"Grandma," I cried, "You're speaking Russian!"

"No, I'm not," she said, decisively.

"Yes, you are," I replied, just as decisively.

"Impossible," she said, in Yiddish, and retreated to her room. I never figured out whether speaking Russian brought back bad memories or whether, sixty years after coming to America, she had truly forgotten that she was once fluent in the language.

Two generations later I responded to Russia's pull. And strangely, Grandma didn't object, didn't warn me off. I believe she was even proud of me for learning Russian. She died in 1969, two months short of her hundredth birthday. When she died, my career was just beginning to take off. I wonder, what would she think of her granddaughter, who made fifty trips to Russia in fifty years?

So here I was, a child who disliked censorship and distrusted Communists, admired eloquent advocates of free speech, and came to learn that her country was not, after all, perfect. A child who loved to read and whose deep fascination with monuments led her to seek their true meaning. A Jewish American child, connected to the Russian Empire in troubling ways through family, simultaneously repelled by and attracted to the place that for the first fifty years of her life was the Soviet Union. It's hard to imagine two places more ideologically different from each other than Hyde Park and the Soviet Union.

CHAPTER 2

MY RUSSIAN PLANET

My love affair with Russia began when I was fourteen, but I'd been working up to it for a few years. Papa had been to Moscow and Leningrad several times in connection with the founding of the journal he created and edited, *Current Anthropology*. He was traveling all over the world in the 1950s, meeting with local anthropologists to talk about the journal, which was to be a scholarly cooperative project. Papa had a penchant for creating social inventions for doing things in original ways, and he was trying to form a worldwide scientific network of anthropologists. He wrote letters to the family from every country he visited, and these letters, written with carbon copies that turned your fingers purple, doubled as his field notes. I read them all eagerly. Egypt, Peru, Ethiopia—I was fascinated by all the countries he visited. But the Soviet Union, particularly Russia, was the only country that spoke to me in sweet siren tones and also frightened me, an irresistible combination.

From early childhood, I perceived the Soviet Union as a different planet from my own. Grandma's Russia was in the past, when we all resided on one planet. She and Grandpa had emigrated, along with millions of others who left various empires around the world for America. They stayed a few years on the Lower East Side of Manhattan and ended up in New Glarus, Wisconsin. The Yiddish-speaking Katz family, fleeing pogroms in the Russian Empire, fit right in. Grandma and Grandpa Tax fled too and settled in Milwaukee, where they and their extended family lived happily. The Chicago in which I grew up was filled with immigrants from the Slavic lands, especially Poland, and from Ireland, Germany, Central America, and many other countries. These were my neighbors; they had come from my planet, and I felt comfortable with them.

But twenty-five years before I was born, the Russian Empire was replaced by the Soviet Union, and the borders were closed. The Soviet leadership also closed the borders of the countries they dominated, and a huge chunk of Eastern and Central Europe and Central Asia was isolated from me, from us in America, from the countries surrounding it. By the time I was fourteen, America had lost touch with that part of our planet, which had, for all practical purposes, become its own planet. America and the Soviet Union were engaged in the Cold War, and we both had nuclear weapons. My school and schools all across the United States had special drills for all the pupils on "Duck and Cover Day," when we heard sirens and learned to cower under our desks. I found it frightening: a piece of our planet had been ripped off by powerful and dangerous forces and was now whirling around in space, its own moons surrounding it. The world from which so many Americans had emigrated was lost to us forever, I thought. The Irish people in Chicago, the Greeks, the Italians, the Mexicans, the Germans from the west of their country—they could all visit the lands of their ancestors. I had classmates who did this from time to time. But those of us whose people had come from the Soviet sphere could not, and it was hard, if not impossible, to keep up with our relatives and friends there: we were now on separate planets.

My love affair with Russian, however, was launched in the summer of 1956, on the University of Pennsylvania campus in Philadelphia. The congress of the International Union of Anthropological and Ethnological Sciences was being held there, and I was looking forward to meeting my first Soviet Russians. I had been at the fringes of anthropological gatherings all my life and enjoyed being a "conference kid." This time, I took special delight in the conference program, even putting my favorite paper titles together into a "scholarly paper," to Papa's amusement.

I certainly wasn't interested in attending sessions, though: I had a book to read. One lovely, sunny day I found myself a bench on a University of Pennsylvania quadrangle and settled down with that book. There the three Soviet anthropologists found me, deeply immersed in an abridged paperback edition of *War and Peace*—in English, of course. I can't imagine today why I was reading an abridged version, as I've always been so strongly opposed to abridgments. Perhaps this was the only paperback edition that I was able to find in the bookstores, relatively lightweight and good for traveling from Chicago to Philadelphia. I'm pretty sure my parents owned a hardcover translation; maybe I felt it wasn't "cool" to lug around such big, heavy books. I felt a little ashamed to be seen carrying this volume, which didn't express the true me, but I was determined to read it anyway.

One of the three men—I. I. Potekhin (a prominent African specialist, I learned later)—asked what I was reading, and I showed him my book. He took it, examined it, and fixed me with a frown. (I was more than a little apprehensive, these being the first Soviet citizens I'd ever met, and I didn't know yet what sort of creatures they were.) Then he gave me a brief but devastating lecture, the main points of which were that I should not be reading an abridged version of Tolstoy's great classic and that in any case I should read it in Russian, not in English.

"Go!" he thundered (or so it seemed to me). "Learn Russian and read *War and Peace*, the whole thing, as it should be read, in its glorious original language."

These injunctions, from a terrifying Soviet authority, were like a punch in my fourteen-year-old stomach. My ears rang, and I felt breathless; I nodded and responded in a small voice that I would learn Russian, and I would read *War and Peace*, all of it, in the original. And I did. On that bench in Philadelphia I fell in love with the Russia of *War and Peace* and was drawn to it despite my fear of the Soviet Union.

But first came Germany, a kind of bridge for me between my American and Russian planets. I came to Russia the first time from Germany, and before I fell in love with Russia, I had begun a relationship with the German language and with Germany—not a love affair but a very deep and solid friendship that has lasted for decades and been immensely important in my life as a scholar of Russia.

I was very comfortable with German; it was one of our family's foreign languages, along with Spanish and Yiddish. Mama had majored in German at the University of Wisconsin in the 1920s and was certified to teach it, although she never did. Susan had also studied German at Lab School and had gone off to Vienna for a summer on the Experiment in International Living when she was sixteen.

When I was sixteen, my parents encouraged me to join others in my German class on a historic summer trip to the Federal Republic of Germany (FRG), known in common parlance as West Germany, as opposed to the German Democratic Republic (GDR), known as East Germany. The trip was led by our inestimable teacher, Herr Gregor Heggen. It was 1958, and we were, apparently, the first American high-school group to visit West Germany after World War II, and grown-ups on both sides of the Atlantic made much of us. The president of the FRG, Dr. Theodor Heuss, visited Chicago before we left for Germany, and we presented him with a bouquet; the Chicago newspapers wrote us up then and again upon our return.

Many of my classmates were Jewish, and apparently our imminent visit created considerable interest among groups in West Germany eager to deal with the recent past. We were welcomed by Jewish-Christian societies in several towns and by organizations supporting international contacts among young people. When word got out that I was signed up for the trip, I remember that my parents were criticized severely and with considerable emotion by some friends and relations: "How can you send her to live with Nazis?" Mama and Papa replied that we would be living with families who knew we were Jewish and who wanted their own children to know us. How could the world move beyond the Holocaust (although I don't think they used that term then), they argued, if the children born in both countries in 1942, too young to have participated in atrocities, couldn't see one another as human beings?

During our ten weeks in West Germany in that summer of 1958, my classmates and I sank and swam, sank and swam in the sea of language—German as spoken by ordinary people in ordinary life conditions. I had a nightmare the night before we left Amsterdam for Germany—amusing now, terrifying then—that I arrived at the home of my new family in Bielefeld and realized that they spoke only Sanskrit, a language I didn't know at all and hadn't even realized was spoken anywhere. My waking self insisted that Sanskrit was a dead language. Not in my dream, though; the family was chattering away in Sanskrit. All that German study for nothing: what a joke on me!

Despite some minor failures, Herr Heggen's solid training paid off: my comprehension and spoken German improved enormously during that summer. I also read a lot of German works and translations into German and was introduced to Françoise Sagan's enormously popular novel *Bonjour Tristesse* and to Anne Frank's diary through German translations. My German friends knew about Sagan, but I may have introduced them to Anne Frank.

I experienced my first encounter with the Iron Curtain in one of its many forms—a barbed wire fence with a no-man's-land ditch and gun towers on the other side—in the summer of 1958. During a bus tour with our Chicago and German school groups, we drove through the Harz Mountain region of West Germany along the border with East Germany. At one point, we were close enough to see the uniforms and faces of the very young GDR soldiers manning those towers, their rifles glinting in the brilliant sunshine. I had never imagined that boys my own age might be armed with deadly weapons, and I recall the frisson I felt when I realized they were pointed at me!

I loved the experience of my summer in Germany so much that I opted to return the following summer, as a student leader of Herr Heggen's second group, between my senior year at University High and my first year at the University of Chicago. My second summer was as engrossing, challenging, and rewarding as the first. This time we spent a week in Berlin, living again with families. We spent most of the week in West Berlin, which was situated on our planet but on an island surrounded completely by the other planet. We traveled by train through the *Ostzone*, the landmass of the GDR, to get to West Berlin from West Germany, crossing a very scary border patrolled by unsmiling guards. The train belonged to the GDR railroad, a state enterprise (like all enterprises on the other planet), and signs throughout the train warned us that destruction of state property was a major crime. This was sobering news for me, as I was intent on bringing a souvenir spoon or two back to Esslingen in West Germany for my friend Stefan, who collected exotic spoons, and I now understood that everything on this planet, large or small, important or insignificant, was state property. (I've changed the names of my German friends.)

In 1959 one could cross from West Berlin into East Berlin quite freely, through certain train stations, and wander around the streets and shops. I don't remember how we got GDR money to buy things; our West Berlin "siblings" (again, we were staying with families) must have known how to do that. Books were incredibly cheap and beautiful, but there wasn't much else that people from our planet would want to buy. Men, women, and children looked different: their clothes were shabbier and less stylish, and their faces were closed in a way that was new to me. I remember feeling uneasy there; people stared at my clothes and shoes, stylish for Western teenagers but definitely out of place in East Berlin.

I was especially uneasy the first time several of us crossed the border, this time by *U-Bahn* (underground train). My usual nervousness exploded into panic, thanks to an acutely embarrassing event that still brings on a cold sweat every time I remember it. I'm seventeen years old, wearing a pretty new skirt and, underneath, a favorite pair of shiny red nylon panties. It's a warm summer day, so I'm bare-legged. Right there in the crowded station, the elastic waistband snaps, and the panties begin their descent. I contort my body and whisper the bad news to my girlfriends, who promptly cluster tightly around me, giving me cover to slither out of the offending panties and slip them into a garbage can. I'm so grateful this was the 1950s, before the age of the minidress!

All three summers, and on many subsequent visits to Germany, I talked with Germans of all ages about being Jewish. In 1958 I had several conversations with Herr Karl Schmidt and his Bielefeld family, who were churchgoing Catholics. Herr Schmidt was a lawyer, a gentle and intelligent man of whom I became very fond. He talked frankly with me about the Nazi era, explaining that he had joined the Nazi Party when he realized that he had to in order to keep his job. With a wife and two small daughters to provide for, he felt he had no choice. He knew that Jewish neighbors lost their homes and eventually disappeared, but he didn't know their ultimate fate; he revealed that he had always been uncomfortable about his passivity, especially when he learned the full story of what had happened to the Jews. He was so pleased that his family now had the opportunity to take me into their home and lives, and I assured him that I understood—and I think I did understand—if not the big picture, the destruction of European Jewry, then the little one of a decent man and his family. I've never judged Herr Schmidt. I've asked myself many times what I would have done in his place, and each time I conclude that I simply don't know.

I didn't judge any of the Germans I met, although I was prepared to if they were judging me because I was Jewish. I never actually had that experience, although some of my classmates did. Over the years I developed a technique to use in case I were to meet such a person. For instance, whenever I found myself riding a German train, I would strike up a conversation with other passengers in my compartment. (I confess that I enjoyed their surprise when they learned that I wasn't a native speaker; I was proud of my German!) If any of the passengers looked old enough to have experienced World War II as an adult, I made sure to mention, early in our conversation, that I was Jewish, visiting from America. I counted on heading off any anti-Semitic statements that might come out of someone's mouth, and indeed, I never did hear any.

I had two host families in 1958, the Schmidts in Bielefeld and the Ecksteins in Esslingen. Herr Eckstein was a house painter; Frau Eckstein was a plump, cheerful woman who cooked the most wonderful regional dishes, spätzle (small pasta dumplings) being my favorite. Like the Schmidts, the Ecksteins were delighted to have me with them, and they provided me with a Jewish experience I've never forgotten. They arranged for me to meet probably the only Jewish couple they knew, local shopkeepers. The husband and wife, both Polish survivors, had met in a concentration camp. They invited me to their home several times, and on one of my visits they showed me the numbers on their arms. I knew about numbers, but I'd never seen any. They reached out to me with an intensity that made me uncomfortable; they had a son, and perhaps they fancied me as a future daughter-in-law. Although they weren't happy in Germany, they didn't seem to have the option of moving elsewhere. Their bitterness and their separateness from the German community in which they lived really troubled me. I felt terribly sorry for them, but when I was with them, I just wanted to be back with the Ecksteins. My life was simpler with my German host families than with those tormented survivors.

Earlier in the summer, at the request of a city father in Herr Heggen's hometown of Paderborn, I had translated into English a short history of the Jewish community. I remember weeping as I worked on the last paragraphs of that document, describing the destruction of the Jewish community by the Nazis. In Bielefeld and Esslingen, and later in Berlin and other German cities, the plight of the Jews was real to me: I saw the houses and shops they used to own, the sites of their ruined synagogues. Through the years my German friends always made sure I saw these places and any memorials erected after the war. They haunt me, and at the same time I'm so glad they are there, preserved for future generations.

GARDEN OF BROKEN STATUES TOUR, STOP 4: BERLIN

The city of Berlin, which I had visited before, during, and after the wall, has become one gigantic and well-documented symbol—a garden of museums, open-air displays, and memorials. In May 2000, back in Berlin for a conference, I tried to capture a few of the city's perspectives with my camera. **Die neue Wache, a nineteenth-century monument built on Unter den Linden Strasse, the Fifth Avenue of Berlin, to celebrate German imperial glory, had a new plaque, installed after 1989, detailing successive generations of victims from the Nazi and Soviet eras.**

In another part of the city, a German friend gave Harvey and me a walking tour of a neighborhood, quiet and pleasant, where many Jews had lived. The city had affixed small plates to paving stones in front of the entrances to some buildings. On these plates we read the names of family members who had lived in a particular apartment, the date on which the Gestapo took them away, and the concentration camps where they died. Nearby, banners were affixed to lampposts, each one giving the text of one of the "anti-Jewish Laws" of 1933–1939 and the dates on which they went into effect: "Jüdische Ärzte dürfen nicht mehr praktizieren *(Jewish doctors are no longer permitted to practice"). 25.7.1938."*

A few blocks away, on the square in front of the Humboldt University Library in former East Berlin (capital of the GDR), a memorial, installed in 1994–1995, by the artist Micha Ullmann, commemorates the Nazi book burning of May 1933. I had a hard time trying to take a picture of this unique memorial: I couldn't get the angle right. It's a glass-covered hole in the ground through which I could see, in the earth below, a chamber filled with empty book-stack units. The plaque quotes a familiar and prescient stanza of a poem that Heinrich Heine wrote in 1820:

Das war ein Vorspiel nur, dort
Wo man Bücher verbrennt,

Verbrennt man am Ende auch Menschen
(That was just a prelude, Where books are burned,
There, in the end, people will be burned too)[1]

In the fall of 1959 I found myself with six other students in a classroom at the University of Chicago, hidden away on the fourth floor of the Classics Building. There the sounds of Russian captivated me as I struggled to master its verbs and the sound of the letter Щ, transliterated into our alphabet as "shch." My first Russian-language teacher was a striking young blonde émigré from the Soviet Union married to a handsome American: so romantic, I thought! She told us to pronounce this letter like "fresh cheese," and I spent the first weekend of the academic quarter memorizing the Cyrillic alphabet, writing the letters over and over, and muttering "fresh cheese" to myself.

According to plan, I returned to Germany for the third consecutive summer in 1960 and spent the first six weeks translating *Mythos und Kult*. The first week I stayed at a little hotel in Frankfurt, meeting with Professor Jensen and his assistant at the professor's University of Frankfurt office. Then I moved to Esslingen, a charming medieval town near Stuttgart, where I had lived with the Ecksteins during my first summer in Germany. This time I lived with Stefan, one of my close friends, his mother, and his younger brother, Wolfgang. I had had a schoolgirl crush on Stefan since my first summer in Germany, when he was a leader of the group that hosted our group in Esslingen. No wonder: he was tall, blond, blue-eyed, handsome. I'm glad to report that our friendship survived my crush, and we're friends to this day.

Esslingen turned out to be a wonderful place for me to live and work on the book. The family rose very early, before 5 a.m., and left the house for work and school. I breakfasted with them and was at my typewriter (I think Stefan rented a Royal for me) by 5. I worked nonstop until noon, when I went out for a walk and lunch—cheese, sausage, and a fine hard roll, all bought at neighborhood shops. By the end of the summer I had perfected my very rudimentary knowledge of the metric system and sampled many delicious sandwiches. My hosts came home later in the afternoon, and we spent the rest of the day pleasantly together. I remember assisting Stefan's

---

1   Heinrich Heine, "Almansor," in *Sämtliche Werke*, vol. 2 (Munich: Winkler Verlag, 1969), 859 (my translation).

mother with jam making, and Wolfgang taught me all about the latest models of German cars; he was especially fond of Mercedes and BMWs. June and July passed happily and productively: hard work tempered by sausage, cheese, cars, walks through historic Esslingen, and harmless flirtation. I completed most of the first draft of my translation and then set off to meet my own family for what I think of as My Great Adventure: August on the Other Planet.

Mama, Papa, Susan, and I met in Prague, where we spent the first days of our month touring Russia, Poland, Hungary, and Yugoslavia, with a brief stop in the GDR. Papa had arranged meetings with local scholars in nine cities in the region. Moscow was our second stop, followed by Warsaw and Krakow, East Berlin, Budapest, Belgrade, Zagreb, and Ljubljana. Everywhere we were hosted by anthropologists, and everywhere I soaked up the atmosphere and struggled to understand each country on this whirlwind tour.

I knew most about Russia and the Soviet Union—I had one year of Russian-language study under my belt and had done quite a bit of reading on my own—but still I knew painfully little about its language and culture. Fortunately, I was aware of my ignorance at every turn. (Living in Germany had taught me humility!) And I knew enough about postwar history to realize that speaking Russian or German—my best languages other than English—might not be such a good idea in this part of the world. I worried particularly that I might offend Poles and Hungarians by those two hated languages, as I knew they had no love for either country, having been occupied so recently by one or the other or both—and the Soviet military was still in Budapest. But what to do if a Pole knew no English? I asked one of our Polish hosts, in hesitant Russian, and was assured, with a warm smile, that any language was better than none, and from then on we spoke Russian together.

Budapest, four years after the failed uprising against the Soviets, had the feel of an occupied city. We saw a woman spit at a Soviet soldier's back, and here and there we encountered little shrines laid against walls pockmarked by bullets. Luckily for me, most of the Hungarians I encountered spoke at least minimal English, but here too I fell back occasionally on Russian or German in order to communicate.

All the cities we visited were fascinating, but for me Moscow was the jewel in the socialist crown and the most exotic destination I could imagine. There were very few Americans in Eastern Europe then and certainly not many in Moscow; although I had experienced the other planet a little bit, at the border between the two Germanys and in East Berlin, flying east I felt as though I had left our planet completely behind, hurtling through space to land, finally, in Moscow, capital of the other planet, a deeply exciting place of mystery and unease.

While Papa was attending meetings, Mama, Susan, and I were sent on tours with the families of other congress participants. That week I was introduced to some of Moscow's wonders: Red Square, St. Basil's, the Kremlin, Moscow State University, the Bolshoi Theater, the Tretyakov Gallery, the great nineteenth-century department store GUM, Lenin's tomb.

We were staying at the recently completed Hotel Ukraina, one of the seven "wedding cake" skyscrapers built around Moscow on Stalin's orders. Once we left our rooms, we tried to stay out for as much of the day as possible, since our parents' room was on one high floor, ours on another, and there were only two impossibly slow and undependable elevators. When you finally got up or down, you stayed there as long as you could hold out.

Relying on my rudimentary Russian, Susan and I went out exploring, alone—no guide. This was frowned upon by Intourist, the state tourist agency charged with looking after visitors, but we simply did it. The weather was gorgeous that August. We wandered the streets, our shoes and clothes marking us as foreigners and attracting constant stares, unsmiling but not unfriendly. One day, hungry, we stopped in a cafeteria on the lower level of a building and filled our plates at various stations along the steam table. When we got to the end, we held out a handful of ruble notes. I don't recall whether someone took money from us or whether we ended up with a free lunch; I realize now that we must have been in the workers' canteen in some kind of institute housed in that building, and they probably didn't pay cash for their food. In any case, it was hot and tasty and much faster than the meals we shared with our parents in more formal settings.

Our most memorable meal en famille was a dinner in the venerable Hotel Natsional near Red Square. Every dish we attempted to order from the gigantic menu was met with a definitive "no" from the unsmiling, indifferent waiter who spent the evening assiduously avoiding our entreating glances. "We don't have that," he would announce in a bored tone each time we made a request. Eventually we concluded that they had only two dishes, one of which we all ordered. When Papa, ever the optimist, ventured to ask about apple dumplings, displayed prominently on the menu, the waiter nodded. We were overjoyed, anticipating dessert.

The meal, not including dessert, lasted about three hours and was mostly spent waiting for each beverage, soup, salad, and entrée to be wheedled out of the reluctant waiter. I was amused to see that Papa, usually an extremely impatient man, was treating the situation as an anthropologist should: it was fieldwork. Mama, who had been through years of such experiences with him (and who was a genuinely patient person), was stoic. Susan and I giggled as quietly and decorously as we could. We had been waiting for perhaps half an hour for the dumplings when the waiter sauntered over and announced haughtily that there were no apples.

On the Russian planet we spent our days among aliens who looked like us but whose world was definitely not ours. Come to think of it, Moscow was perhaps a little like Disneyland: all activities were organized for visitors by the ubiquitous Intourist guides, men and women who spoke languages well and were employed by the official tourist agency to introduce foreigners to the country. I learned later that they had been vetted carefully for dependability and loyalty to the state and could be counted on to keep a proper distance from the aliens while presenting a friendly face.

The scenes in front of which the guides gave their spiels were splendid, dazzling to the eye: Stalin's seven imposing skyscrapers dotting the horizon; Red Square, complete with Lenin's tomb and a Red Army honor guard in parade dress; the stunning Technicolor backdrop of St. Basil's Cathedral. Disneyland is pleasant indeed, but you know it's not the real world; you must leave the Magic Kingdom to see the scowls on people's faces, the litter on the streets of Anaheim. Intourist didn't show us the real world of Moscow either; away from that picturesque, colorful center stretched mile after mile of shabby apartment houses, shops with empty shelves, solemn-faced people.

My first friend in the Soviet Union was Vladimir, a handsome, rather dashing young anthropologist whom I met during the week in Moscow. A young colleague of none other than my Philadelphia anthropologist of

War and Peace fame, Vladimir was around forty and definitely the romantic "older man" in my eighteen-year-old eyes. He had come to Moscow from Leningrad, where he lived, to participate in the Sixth International Congress of Anthropological and Ethnological Sciences and had been assigned to take us around, although at the time I thought, naively, that he just enjoyed the pleasure of our family's company, especially that of Susan and me. An Africanist like his senior professor, Vladimir had received his doctorate from Leningrad State University. His English was pretty fluent, but once he realized that I was studying Russian, he was good about engaging me in conversation. To my romance-seeking eighteen-year-old sensibilities, he was a hero out of Russian literature: dark-haired, intense, a bit moody. I believe he had been married and divorced; at that time I knew very few divorced people, and this added to his exotic aura. As I recall, he had one or two gold or silver teeth, which enhanced his foreign appearance. (I hadn't heard about the horrors of Soviet dentistry yet and still thought metal teeth were cool.)

When we left Moscow, Vladimir gave me a small icon, urging me not to show anyone, as such items were not allowed out of the country. This icon brought on the first of many bouts of anxiety suffered when dealing with Soviet—and later, Russian—customs, but in fact I've never had trouble at airports, although travelers around me certainly have. I brought the icon home and kept it for years but now can't find it; we may have given it away. I have no idea whether it was old, valuable, or interesting in any way, but it always reminded me of Vladimir.

Back in Chicago, I struck up a correspondence with him, composing for him little stories in the style of Chekhov (my favorite Russian author) and sending them to him. He was a fine and tactful editor, correcting my mistakes without offending me and giving me just enough praise to keep me going. I wish I had kept our correspondence and those stories, but they are all gone, felled by a wave of housecleaning. I don't have a picture of Vladimir, but I see him clearly in my mind, although I'm not sure about the metal teeth; I may be mixing him up with dozens, probably hundreds, of other men I saw subsequently.

But Papa's letters and field notes—closely written paragraphs, filling every inch of each page of hotel stationery—mentioned Vladimir and what happened to him. There's quite a bit about Vladimir, mostly in letters from

Papa's 1963 trip, when he spent a few days in Leningrad and was with Vladimir for several hours. As I read, I was distressed by facts that didn't mean much, or anything, to me then. Papa learned from one of the senior people that Vladimir was in trouble professionally; he had lost his temper and told off his party committee at a meeting when they rejected his request to travel to England. I don't remember what my reaction was when I first read about this event, but I'm sure I didn't understand its significance. By June 1963 I certainly should have known enough about life in the Soviet Union to realize how serious this was. As I read these words today, after a lifetime studying such things, my eyes fill with tears. Poor, impatient Vladimir! There went his chances to go abroad, to be hired for a permanent position at his institute, to have a better life all around. Some years later I heard that he had died of a heart attack, and I grieved for him; I'll always have a warm spot for Vladimir.

At the end of this remarkable month, I spent a few days with the family near Vienna, at Burg Wartenstein, a medieval castle owned by the Wenner-Gren Foundation, Papa's sponsor for *Current Anthropology*. After decompressing there, I took the train back to Esslingen for a few more weeks. Mama and Papa came to visit, and Stefan helped me write up my impressions from the Soviet and East European trip, in German, for publication in a youth magazine, *Ja und Nein*. I squirm a little as I look at those texts today: I wrote then with the certainty and arrogance of youth. And speaking of the arrogance of youth, I brought Stefan several more spoons for his collection, acquired on my travels through Eastern Europe and the Soviet Union—all state property. I had breathed a sigh of relief each time I passed successfully through customs, spoons intact; as far as I know, these were the only crimes I ever committed in Communist countries.

My family's trip to Eastern Europe and the Soviet Union took place in the middle of the Cold War, albeit during the decade-long "thaw" that set in after Stalin's death in 1953. The thaw had begun in February 1956, when Nikita Khrushchev, Stalin's successor, presented his "secret speech" to delegates to the Twentieth Party Congress and revealed Stalin's crimes officially. I was too ignorant to detect signs of melting while we were in Russia, although I know now that they were visible and palpable to Soviet citizens. I began to understand the thaw over the next few years, when I continued my studies in college and then graduate school, deeply immersed in Russian studies. I recall the excitement of my teachers, many of whom were émigrés who had experienced the pre-thaw Soviet Union. They were thrilled by the changes taking place in intellectual life there, and they infused our classes with heady doses of most welcome cheer. Older graduate students on their way to Moscow or Leningrad for a semester or a year looked forward to living in a friendlier, more open climate.

I suspect that most Americans didn't care about the thaw on the other planet, if they even knew about it. We were busy building highways and suburbs and shopping malls and factories—and bomb shelters. We were rich and secure, but at the same time we worried mightily about containing the Communist world. The Korean War was over; the Vietnam War was on our horizon. But the handful of us who were Russian scholars and budding scholars did care. We watched with enormous interest and excitement as Alexander Solzhenitsyn was allowed to publish his novella *One Day in the Life of Ivan Denisovich*, about a gulag prisoner's life, while real prisoners began to return from the gulag, released by the highest authorities.

From our vantage point in Chicago—and New York, Boston, Berkeley, wherever we Russian scholars were—we could see all kinds of changes, in every area of life, but it all seemed fragile. We were afraid the balloon would burst; after all, the Communist Party remained in charge. And sure enough, in 1964 it ended, when hardliners took over and the ground froze once more. Since then, when I hear or read the word "thaw," whatever the context, I have a melancholy, bittersweet flash: in my mind's eye a thaw comes, the sap flows, people get excited; then the ground freezes and stagnation sets in. It's all over.

My week in Moscow and three weeks in Eastern Europe were incredibly intense: I felt as though I'd been away for a year. I'd studied Russian for one academic year, and I'd actually been in Russia, speaking the language with natives, no matter how clumsily. And they understood me! When the trip was over, I plunged back into my studies. I was hooked, blissfully happy, floating on a cloud of Russia-love. My second-year language teacher was also an émigré, a tiny woman of a certain age with beautiful black hair and sparkling eyes. I adored her. She was elegant, charming, and cultured; her accented English was delightful; and she was so eager to share her pre-Soviet

Russia with us. In the first and second years we worked our way through short stories by Pushkin, Lermontov, Chekhov, Tolstoy, all in Russian. I was enthralled; this was nothing like reading an abridged *War and Peace* in English. My ear and palate picked up the rhythm of the Russian language, and the sounds that had seemed so strange at first (that Щ, for example) began to trip off my tongue. The characters with their double names—Ivan Ivanovich, Nataliia Fedorovna—and their nicknames—Vania, Natasha—became old friends.

The only Jewish native speaker I encountered among my language teachers taught me third-year Russian. Like the others she was an émigré, but I felt a special affinity for her; she might have been my aunt. She told us that to really understand the Russian soul, we must read *Anna Karenina*—in Russian, of course—and write about it. So we wrote halting essays in Russian and tried to penetrate the Russian soul.

Meanwhile, after being introduced to Tchaikovsky's violin concerto in Humanities I, I took to sitting for hours on the floor at home in front of our two enormous Magnavox speakers and let myself be carried away, never mind my ever-scratchier LP recording. From then on I listened to all the Russian music I could find—classical, folk, the Red Army Chorus, Orthodox church liturgy—while working my way through Russian stories, memorizing nouns, struggling with verbs, and plunging into Russian history and culture for my "Russian Civ" course. In the first quarter I fell in love with *byliny*, epic poems of the tenth and eleventh centuries, and developed a fascination with Tsar Ivan the Terrible (better translated as "the Fearsome," or perhaps "the Awesome," in the old sense of that word). For the rest of the year, my teacher was Thomas Riha, a young Czech-born scholar who involved his students in translating short pieces for the course syllabus, later published as *Selected Readings in the History of Russian Civilization*; he also directed the university's Russian chorus, in which I sang.

My contribution to the syllabus was an excerpt from a memoir by a Russian doctor who survived the Leningrad Blockade and wrote dispassionately about its horrors. Translating this piece was a chilling experience, and I learned all I'll ever need to know about the process of starving to death. The chorus, in contrast, was a joy. Riha had directed the Yale Russian Chorus, much more famous than ours, before coming to the University of Chicago.

We gave concerts on campus, and on one memorable occasion, we sang the Easter midnight liturgy in one of Chicago's Russian churches, an amazing and uplifting experience.

A few years later Riha disappeared in a dramatic and bizarre way. Had he been a victim of Soviet intelligence? Was he a spy? There were alleged sightings behind the Iron Curtain. I don't think the mystery has ever been solved, although perhaps his closed file lies in some intelligence service office somewhere in the world.

By the time I graduated, in August 1962, and started graduate school, I was firmly ensconced in Russian heaven, deeply and blissfully engaged with the Russian soul. But as I was splashing happily in my pre-1917 Russian culture bath, I also felt the Soviet chill. We students knew something about Stalin's crimes; our émigré teachers told us stories. My Soviet literature teacher was George Bobrinskoy, a member of an ancient aristocratic Russian family, who had come to the United States in 1923. A professor of Sanskrit and in the Slavic Department as well, Bobrinskoy had us read Socialist-Realist classics, including *Tsement* (Cement) and *Kak zakalialas stal'* (How the Steel Was Tempered), and write analyses in Russian. Reading these works

Marianna with parents on her wedding day (August 28, 1962)

was not easy; I had to immerse myself in Stalin's world and try to understand its realities. The collective over the individual. Glorification of labor and laborers. Absolute loyalty to the party and its supreme leader. If there was poetry in these works or beautiful language and memorable characters, it all eluded me. I yearned for Chekhov, Tolstoy, Pushkin.

Meanwhile, in real life, Sputnik, the space satellite the Soviets launched in 1957—before we, the mighty United States, launched one!—was fresh in our memories. We American graduate students benefited from our country's embarrassment. Generous fellowships came our way, funded by our government and private foundations. We were urged—enticed by those fellowships and, at least in my case, fed by Russia-love—to continue and deepen our studies in history, political science, economics, sociology and anthropology, languages and literatures of the Soviet-ruled region. My fellowship, with its dependents' allowance, supported Harvey and me comfortably in married student housing.

I had fallen in love with imperial Russia, thrown myself into its language, literature, and history. That first visit to the Soviet Union in 1960 had stunned me and complicated my love with a sense of dread, but it didn't deter me. My next trip wasn't until 1978, when I went to Leningrad on University of Illinois Library business. Two years in Bangladesh, surprise twin babies, sojourns at two universities, an unexpected career as a Slavic-specialist librarian, and an even more unexpected connection to Russian and Soviet censorship had kept me away until then, but after that week in Leningrad in 1978, reasons to go to the region, and funding to get me there, kept coming my way, and I became a regular on flights to Moscow and beyond.

The world has changed so drastically. I used to see the Soviet Union and the West as remote planets whose orbits would never intersect except violently, and for as long as I can remember, I believed that. Then, miracle of miracles, in the late 1980s their orbits began to shift, tentatively at first and then with dizzying speed. After the collapse of the Soviet Union at the end of 1991 and through the first decade of post-Soviet Russia, I traveled between the two planets/countries three and four times a year. After that the pace slowed, but I still made one or two visits each year and continue to do so. Especially in the 1990s and the first years of the new century, each trip took me to a changed country, as though someone had shaken a giant kaleidoscope.

What was so exciting about Russia at the beginning of my love affair? Certainly the language, which I had only just begun to penetrate. I loved its cadences and its alphabet, at once familiar and exotic. I wanted so much to master it, and the classroom, where I excelled, was far removed from the streets of Moscow, where I stumbled. What a challenge! Sometimes, when I opened my mouth, German tumbled out, or a mix of German and English, with a few Spanish words from my early childhood mixed in, or a bit of French from my lessons with Barbara Hutchins, or some Yiddish, and I had to struggle to bring Russian words up out of this soup. The effort, the intense concentration required, got my adrenalin flowing. Oddly, I wasn't frustrated, just stimulated, and ever since I've valued that electrifying connection with the Russian language that recurs with each visit.

My heart missed a beat when I first caught sight of St. Basil's, that wildly colored and patterned cluster of onion domes on Red Square. I couldn't take my eyes off it: I had never seen anything like it before, and pictures did not do it justice. Nor did pictures capture the massive elegance of the Kremlin, the sheer size of it, the warm gold of its cupolas. Moscow streets didn't look like Chicago streets: very few cars of makes unknown to me; mostly trucks, khaki-colored military vehicles with big black numbers on their sides.

And the people who thronged the streets on these pleasant August days didn't look like the Americans who thronged my Chicago streets in August. They didn't look like the German crowds with which I was familiar either. They dressed differently from us, they didn't smile much, and those whom we encountered as salespeople in shops and servers in restaurants were striking in their utter indifference to customers. To me, coming from Chicago's Marshall Field and Company, where the motto was "Give the lady what she wants," the Russian total rejection of me, the eager customer, was like a slap in the face.

I felt bemused by all the differences, and I found it exhilarating to be in an environment so different from America or Western Europe. I suppose I had absorbed some of Papa's anthropological attitude. He used to talk about a hypothetical anthropologist from Mars who would observe us Earth people with a dispassionate and not unsympathetic eye and try to understand what we were all about. And here I was, a visitor from my planet observing the other planet for a few days.

Susan became an anthropologist, like Papa. I became a Russian scholar, a Slavic librarian, and perhaps an anthropologist by osmosis, through my deep connection to Papa. Many years later, when I founded the Mortenson Center for International Library Programs and worked with librarians and their communities in Russia and around the world, I was influenced by his *Current Anthropology* activities and by "action anthropology," the field he is credited with founding, in which the scholar helps a community to achieve its own goals and studies that community at the same time. The action anthropologist conducts basic research—studies a people's culture, collects data, builds theory, just as a "regular" anthropologist does—and at the same time helps that people to work toward goals it defines as important. These two aspects of the action anthropologist's work are equally important, and they reinforce each other. There's no conflict between "pure" and "applied"; on the contrary, they are two sides of the same coin.

In 1992 Katia drew me into post-Soviet Russia and the Library for Foreign Literature. She encouraged me to continue my research on censorship while working with her to help librarians in the former Soviet Union meet their new post-Soviet goals, including one goal that many didn't even realize would be important: respect for tolerance and intellectual freedom.

Katia met Papa only once, and they admired each other. I suspect that, had they had opportunities to really get to know each other, they would have discovered that they were kindred souls. For the past twenty years I've practiced "action Russian studies," with Katia as my partner.

GARDEN OF BROKEN STATUES TOUR, STOP 5: BUCHENWALD
Buchenwald is located in picturesque hills just outside Goethe's beautiful city of Weimar, also the site, between the wars, of the short-lived Weimar Republic.

The setting itself is noteworthy: Weimar is in the eastern part of Germany and was thus in the Soviet zone of occupation, which became the German Democratic Republic. The wall surrounding the GDR, what we used to call East Germany, came down in 1989, along with the Berlin Wall. A few isolated symbols of everyday life in the GDR remain along the former border between the two Germanys.

   Our friend Stefan, who grew up in the Federal Republic of Germany, was Harvey's and my guide in August 1998. He had worked for the past few years in the former GDR and knew how to spot these symbols. As we approached Weimar in Stefan's car, he pointed out a couple of them on the busy autobahn near the city of Eisenach: a tower that used to house enormous searchlights and a guardhouse and guard tower, manned in the not-so-distant "old days" by young soldiers searching with their rifle sights for people trying to leave the GDR. The no-man's-land that existed in GDR times to separate the two Germanys is no longer visible; we had to imagine it. There are no historical markers.

A German Democratic Republic watchtower on the former border between East and West Germany, near Eisenach, Germany (August 1998)

The Buchenwald site is a museum and has been one since GDR times. This is what makes it so fascinating for me: the complex layers of history— Nazi, GDR and Soviet, post-Soviet German—each with its own interpretation of "the facts." We enter Buchenwald through an arch, under the cruel Nazi slogan "Jedem das Seine" ("to each his own, to each what he deserves, to each what's coming to him"). After a short walk we come to one of the cellblocks, restored for visitors. The cells along a narrow corridor are furnished as they had been: narrow cot, small table. On the wall, under barred windows, are memorials to the prisoners who lived and died there, such as a Protestant pastor who tried to protect Jews and others and was tortured and executed.

Site of Jewish barracks, Buchenwald Concentration Camp, near Weimar, Germany (August 1998)

We move on to the outer room of the crematorium, dozens of urns stacked neatly under a window, floral arrangements in the foreground. Outside, we spend some minutes at a memorial on the site of the Jewish barracks, an open space covered in rocks, memorial candles, and pebbles (traditional on Jewish graves) left by mourners or passersby.

Then we walk to a large, shallow, circular depression in the ground covered with healthy-looking velvety green grass mowed short, an idyllic spot—until we realize that the beautiful grass blankets the ashes of countless corpses. Rising into the sky beyond the ash pit, outside the camp wall, is a massive brick tower flanked by Socialist-Realist statues, a Soviet-style GDR-era memorial, with a text that recounts the history of this place in Soviet-style distortions.

When Germany was reunified, the Federal Republic of Germany agreed to maintain all GDR monuments as they were, in perpetuity. Good, I say: we need to see the symbols of each stratum as they were then, and we need explanations that place the symbols in that stratum. The post-GDR museum at Buchenwald does this in an exemplary way; we can review all the strata and consider the history of this place in light of the latest historical research.

For me an especially stunning and visceral exhibit at Buchenwald is one that was still under construction when I was there while historical, archeological, and forensic research was still in progress. I'm talking about the forest cemetery a few steps from the camp, where victims of Special Camp (Spetslager) no. 2 are buried. Just after the war, I learn, the Soviets took over the facilities at Buchenwald and set up their own camp, incorporated into the gulag system. Camp personnel went about their business in secret: their prisoners were executed and buried in unmarked mass graves, revealed only after the collapse of the Soviet Union. Research was ongoing when I visited and continues. As bodies are discovered, each is marked with a polished stainless steel pole, an understated but dramatic symbol, German modernist in style, creating a grim forest-within-a-forest in this beautiful, pastoral setting. As we walk in the forest, we tread upon who knows how many bodies.

CHAPTER 3

BANGLADESH AND BABIES

I had always assumed that I would complete my PhD in a few years, certainly by the mid-1960s. First, I'd finish my master's degree—all I lacked was one paper—and then I'd write my dissertation on some topic in Russian literature. Harvey and I would find jobs at a university somewhere. But adventure knocked on our door, and we had a two-year diversion (1964–1965) in, of all places, East Pakistan, now Bangladesh but at that time the tiny, poor stepsister of West Pakistan, located on the other side of gigantic India. Harvey had completed his doctoral exams and was writing his dissertation, which had nothing whatever to do with East Pakistan. Following the advice of his major professor, he agreed to take a job for two years as a researcher on a community development project based at the Pakistan Academy for Rural Development.

I wasn't worried about this interruption to my plans. I would write the paper needed for my master's in East Pakistan; I packed the books I thought I would need and planned to order more from the Victor Kamkin Bookstore in suburban Washington, DC, my regular supplier. We'd be back in the States in 1965, and I'd write the dissertation then. I was twenty-one years old, and a two-year postponement seemed insignificant. While preparing for East Pakistan I had time to audit a Bengali language class at the university. I'd take the class materials with me and find a local teacher. By the time we returned, I'd have Bengali under my belt too. I might find a Bengali-Russian connection: who knows? If anyone had told me what actually lay ahead—premature twins in 1965, master's in 1967, doctorate in 1979—I simply wouldn't have believed it.

We left Chicago on December 14, 1963, and that was the last I saw of winter for two years. Our parents accompanied us to the airport. Mama's final words of advice to me as we walked through the gate to board the plane were: "Use your noodle!" (In our family, using one's noodle meant exercising caution and common sense.) Mama and Papa, veterans of life in the highlands of Guatemala and in Mexico, had warned us about boiling our drinking water, avoiding raw fruits and vegetables that couldn't be peeled, and various other bits of wisdom.

They also suggested that we pack lightly and try living as the locals do. I'm sorry to say that we ignored this last advice and took a different path. The Population Council, Harvey's employer, followed the US government and Ford Foundation model: take with you everything you need to re-create your life in the States, and we'll pay for the shipping. So we packed a lot of things and shipped them. Our boxes sat on the docks in tropical ports for weeks on end awaiting transshipping. Clearly, it rained on those boxes, heavily. By the time they reached us, weeks after we arrived, many household utensils, items of clothing, and—worst of all—books were covered with a sickly sweet-smelling, thick white paste made of wet Tide detergent.

We flew from Chicago to Tokyo, where we spent a glorious week in Frank Lloyd Wright's Imperial Hotel. Then on to Taiwan to visit a family planning project; Hong Kong for three days; a week in Bangkok, then a sleepy and delightful town with practically no traffic; and a few hours in the airport in Rangoon, Burma. We weren't allowed to leave the airport, but we made good use of our time there: I bought some "Rangoon Specials," cigars beloved of a fellow graduate student at the University of Chicago, and mailed them to him from the airport. Finally, just after New Year's, we landed in East Pakistan, our home for the next two years.

I couldn't have found myself in a place more different from Russia, from the Soviet Union, from my graduate work, from the life path on which I thought I was embarked. Yet another planet? No, more like time travel, back to an outpost of the British Raj. I loved it there, basking in the heat and sun of the tropical rainforest, immersed in the intense green of the rice paddy. Near our home were the Buddhist ruins of Mainamati, encompassing a huge territory in the Lalmai ridge of hills. A large Pakistan army base, or cantonment, was located nearby, but you could wander freely through the partially excavated sections of Mainamati and, if you were a romantic like me, dream yourself back to the sixth through thirteenth centuries and imagine your life in this place of culture and beauty.

Different from Russia, yes. Irrelevant? Absolutely not, I realize now. I learned another language, Bengali, and grew comfortable in it, as I had in German. I adjusted to living in another culture, one where women's lives were very different from my own. I shared those lives for several hours each day and worked on understanding, if not accepting, their relationship to men and to the world in which they lived. I got used to being stared at wherever we went, to being perceived as an object of curiosity. I grew accustomed to the sight of absolute poverty. I practiced the art of listening very, very attentively. I cultivated a poker face for those occasions when something shocked me or struck me as funny.

As a young girl I had been fascinated by Islam and bought myself a copy of the Quran (in English, of course), which I read carefully. Now, living in a Muslim country, I learned about Islam in its East Pakistani form from the inside, intimately. One of the things we realized while living there was that religions don't exist in a vacuum; the people who practice them do so within their cultures and their histories, in this case the centuries of Hindu culture that surrounded them. Islam was a newcomer to the Indian subcontinent, arriving in northern India in the twelfth century; Hinduism had been around for millennia already. When I returned to Russian studies, I brought with me a new sensitivity to the complexities of religion, culture, and history.

I also came to realize, through failure, that sometimes it's best to put something aside and come back to it later. While we were in East Pakistan, I made a false start on my master's paper, attempting to write about the novels of a Soviet writer, Vera Panova. Perhaps because I was so far from my sources and from Hugh Maclean, my professor, or because I really didn't like Panova very much, or because I was distracted by my new life—for whatever reason I produced a very bad draft, pounded it out on our little manual typewriter, and mailed it to Maclean, who suggested gently that I wait until I was home and then try again, on a different topic. With relief I put the paper aside. In 1966, back in the United States, I wrote happily and easily about a trilogy of stories—"About Love," "The Man in a Shell," and "Gooseberries"—by an author I truly loved then and still do: Anton Chekhov.

Liberated from that master's paper, I put Russia temporarily on the back burner and threw myself into life in our new home and community. The academy was located on a new campus designed by the prominent Greek architect Constantinos Doxiades, at Kotbari, about five miles from the town of Comilla. Kotbari was some fifty miles from Dhaka (spelled "Dacca" then, but I'll use today's spelling), the capital, by road, but you couldn't get there by road alone. East Pakistan was mostly water, on the Ganges-Brahmaputra delta where the two great rivers come together to empty into the Bay of Bengal. When we drove in the Panama Beige Volkswagen Beetle provided by the Population Council, we had to ford the rivers on two ferries, one large and one scarily small and rickety, with spaces between the floor slats so you could see the churning water below and hear and see the old truck engine that powered the ferry. The trip between Kotbari and Dhaka took between four and five hours. Or we could ride the train, the Green Arrow, and that took even longer, as the tracks went around the rivers somehow.

Our transport of choice was the airbus, a fleet of hardy old DC-3s belonging to Pakistan International Airlines (advertising motto: "Dead on Time!"). These intrepid little machines had flown the Hump—the air route for sending supplies from India to China—during World War II, taking off and landing on our local airfield, built for the purpose in the jungle. By the time we got there, the jungle had taken the airfield back, except for one runway, and even it had goats that munched on the greenery. Our planes flew to Dhaka once a day except for Tuesdays, when they flew to Kathmandu, in Nepal. We always meant to fly to Kathmandu some Tuesday, but invariably something got in the way, and we never did get there. I dream of it still.

Our favorite plane in the small fleet was patched together the long way, from nose to tail, out of two planes. Inside, the wall and ceiling along one side was green and the other side was pink. Occasionally we flew in the queen of the fleet, a Fokker Friendship, in which the cabin hung below the wings. The flight was faster, but I preferred our colorful, beat-up little DC-3.

The flights were rarely smooth—we didn't fly very high, and the winds could be quite strong, especially during the monsoon season—but although I often felt queasy, I was never afraid. And we flew so close to the ground!

We traveled to Dhaka about once a month, staying with new American friends who worked for the University of California on a Ford Foundation contract. Our main entertainment in the city, aside from the occasional movie, was shopping for some food items we missed sorely; we loved Bengali food and ate it happily, but once in a while we craved the taste of home, such as cheese, which is not part of the Bengali diet. Sometimes we shopped at Dhaka's public market, sometimes at a shop known as Whispering Willie's, whose stock, it was rumored, had fallen off the back of trucks carrying supplies for expats and landed on Willie's shelves.

With the canned cheese from Denmark, I baked pizzas in my little kerosene oven for us and for the small group of Peace Corps volunteers who lived and worked in Comilla and Kotbari. I made my own dough, thanks to the dry yeast packets Mama sent in letters from Chicago, and it rose in a matter of minutes when I left the bowl on a chair in the tropical sun. (Once a stray dog made short work of my dough, and I had to find a less accessible sunny spot.) I formed the pizzas on flat aluminum pot lids, the only utensils small enough to fit into the oven. It took a long time to make enough pizzas for us, but we didn't mind.

The Peace Corps volunteers became our close friends; we were all about the same age. There was a nurse, a librarian, a dairy expert from Vermont, and a young man who was supposed to teach "shop" at a local school, although without electricity for the power tools sent through an aid program, it was slow going for him. The only other Americans around were a family of Baptist missionaries, a group of nuns who ran a school, and an older couple in charge of a Ford Foundation project. A middle-aged English woman ran a literacy program, and there were two Japanese rice experts. Of course, there were many more foreigners in Dhaka, and we got to know one family quite well, staying with them when we were in the city. But in Comilla and Kotbari we were a small minority, and that was fine.

When we wanted a real break beyond Dhaka, every few months we flew to Calcutta, the nearest metropolis. True city people, we really missed the feel of a big city. Kotbari was definitely rural, and Dhaka struck us as an overgrown village. A trip to Calcutta meant crossing the Indian-Pakistani border, which required a more substantial plane, and we felt like international travelers, which was just what we needed. And we fell in love with Calcutta, a marvelous city that reminded us somehow of Chicago: it had the same bustle, the same urban energy. We ate sumptuous meals at Firpo's, where there were a half-dozen turbaned waiters for each diner, watching you like a hawk in case your napkin slipped off your lap. For more modest and lively meals we went to the Blue Fox, shining brightly in my memory as the place where, for the first and perhaps last time in my life, I won a raffle. My prize, a thermos bottle, brought to mind Grandma, the only other family member who had ever won a raffle; her prize was a toaster, which we used for years. The thermos bottle returned to Kotbari with us.

I continued my Bengali lessons with the wife of one of Harvey's colleagues; both husband and wife became close friends. Although she protested that she didn't know how to teach languages, I responded that I knew very well how to learn them and would guide her. Together we did a passable job, and by the time I left East Pakistan, I was quite fluent in reading and comprehension; my spoken Bengali was a little rough, but I could get by.

Doxiades had designed comfortable bungalows for the academy faculty, with smaller bungalows for staff and even more modest little row houses for the lowest level of workers. Our bungalow wasn't ready when we arrived, so for the first eight months we lived in two adjacent dormitory rooms converted for us into a small but functional apartment. One bedroom became our living room, and its bathroom was transformed into our kitchen. It was a strange, windowless room with the toilet still in place, covered by a flat piece of wood.

Our dorm neighbors were civil servants from all over East Pakistan who came for various periods to attend short courses. We didn't get to know these men and women who came and went quite frequently—I often wondered what they made of us, the young American couple in their odd apartment—but gradually we did become close friends with several of Harvey's colleagues on the faculty. Most of the men, and one unmarried woman, had master's degrees from British or American universities. None of the wives had studied abroad, although a number of them did have bachelor's and master's degrees from colleges and universities in Pakistan.

Even though they seemed rather "Westernized," we soon realized that these couples were different from us in significant ways. Most had had arranged marriages, and men and women did not socialize together. I spent most of my time with the women, wives of the academy faculty among whom we lived. They accepted me graciously into their circle and—a great compliment—gently ignored me while they went about their own socializing. My Bengali comprehension skills improved dramatically from my hours spent with the women, and soon I became brave enough to speak a little. When I did, they were so proud of me! And when our bungalow was finally ready, the women gave us a proper Bengali housewarming party. They painted my feet with henna and brought appropriate sweets, sang, and chattered. We women gathered at one end of the living room, while the men crowded together at the other end. We were finally launched as members of their local society.

I loved that bungalow. We had furnished our home carefully, exactly as our neighbors did, buying handmade furniture from the same sources in Comilla to which they directed us. We refused to install air conditioners, although Harvey's employer urged us to do so. The neighbors helped us direct our one servant, a boy named Abdul, whom we had hired on the advice of the English woman who ran a local literacy project. Abdul was a pretty good cook, as soon as he realized that we wanted to eat Bengali food and not what he called "English," tasteless, colorless fare that we choked down for a couple of days only. He had managed very well in the bathroom/kitchen and was now delighted to have his own real kitchen. Sometimes he slept on the floor of that kitchen.

Abdul shopped every day at the market—this was men's work, and only the occasional foreign woman was to be seen there—and brought home live chickens and all kinds of fruits and vegetables, some familiar and many strange for us. Aside from Abdul's habit of killing chickens for dinner while we were eating lunch—I simply couldn't stand the squawking and made him stop—and his initial unwillingness to clean toilets, we got along beautifully. I explained that in my country, I cleaned the toilets myself and showed him how to do it. From then on, we understood each other. Like our neighbors, we employed only one servant, plus a *dhobi*, a Hindu laundry man who came once a week and took our clothes away to wash and iron them. We were amused when he asked us for a Christmas bonus and pointed out to him that he was a Hindu, we were Jews, and we lived in a Muslim country. Of course, we gave him a small gift anyway.

I became accustomed to wearing a sari, pulled over my head for modesty and invisibility when I was out and about, and Harvey wore cotton slacks and shirts, as his colleagues did. Some wore the local men's outfit, a wide white cotton pajama and a long, loose white cotton overshirt called a Punjabi. Harvey wore his only on special occasions. With our dark hair and my native dress, we looked to the locals rather like a couple from the northwestern part of the Indian subcontinent or the Middle East, where people are taller and have fairer skin than is typical of Bengalis. We discovered that some of the academy staff referred to us as "the Egyptian brother and sister," because we walked side by side rather than with Harvey in the lead, as was the local custom. We ate magnificently, having fallen in love with Bengali cuisine, and we lapped up as much culture as we could, while at the same time listening to a new group called the Beatles on Radio Australia's shortwave world broadcast.

During our first year, Papa popped in to visit us. He was headed somewhere in our part of the world on *Current Anthropology* business—I can't remember where—and arrived bearing kosher salami from Chicago and fresh cheese from Denmark, where he had changed planes. He met Akhter Hameed Khan, our community development project's charismatic leader, and became very enthusiastic about what was going on in Comilla.

We were to stay two years in East Pakistan, but I became pregnant in September 1964, and life took a sharp turn, as it so often does. My friend who was also my Bengali teacher had gotten pregnant a few months earlier, and both of our doctors were in Dhaka. She would give birth in a maternity clinic used by upper-class Bengalis. I was a patient of Sister Luke, an American Catholic missionary obstetrician based at Holy Family Hospital, a medical missionary order based in Philadelphia. Sister Luke was stern but kind, with a round face lit up occasionally by a warm smile. She was extremely concerned about overweight mothers-to-be and insisted that I drop thirty pounds in the course of my pregnancy. She terrified me with her stories of how dangerous it was for both mother and baby for the mom to be overweight, and I dreaded my monthly weigh-ins. I ate very carefully, cut down on salt, and gained not an ounce during my pregnancy: Sister Luke's frown was something to be reckoned with.

Early in my pregnancy we made a trip to West Pakistan to visit friends, a couple about our own age whom we had met at the University of Chicago. When they returned to Lahore, they urged us to visit them during our stay in East Pakistan. I'll call them Ahmed and Aishah, and they were a handsome couple. Aishah wore exquisite saris and *shalwar-kameez* outfits (loose-fitting pants with a long tunic worn over them and a *dupatta*, or scarf, around the shoulders) and gold jewelry. They spoke a beautiful, lightly accented British English that we later identified as the language of educated Pakistanis and Indians.

Ahmed and Aishah met our plane in Lahore and showed us their native city, of which they were very proud—just as we were proud of Chicago. We stayed in their well-appointed home for a couple of days and then set out on a car trip that Harvey and I will never forget. We were on the road for about a week, heading north and west to Rawalpindi and Peshawar, with a side trip to the Swat Valley, which was at that time a tribal state within Pakistan. I think I remember our friends telling us that Swat was one of the world's leading centers for emerald mining, and I either recall or imagine that I held some uncut emeralds in my hands. I'm sure we didn't buy any emeralds, but we do have a lovely little textile from Swat, and when I look at it, I think about that exotic place.

We spent a memorable day at what must be one of the world's greatest flea markets, in Landi Kotal in the Khyber Pass, a short distance from the Afghanistan border. You could buy or trade for just about anything there: carpets, electronics large and small, weapons large and small. No questions asked about provenance and lots of bargaining. We bought a carpet as a wedding present for my sister, and then Ahmed told us that one of the local men—heavily armed, as they all were, with rifles and knives—offered to trade something for me. I don't recall what the terms of the trade were, but the idea chilled me. It may have been a joke; I'll never know. But when I see pictures of men in northwest Pakistan and Afghanistan today, armed to the teeth as they were in 1964, I feel that chill again.

At night we stayed in government rest houses (dak bungalows) along the road, and we stopped for meals with relatives of our hosts, all military people stationed in the region. The dak bungalows were comfortable and the families wonderfully hospitable. Memories of that trip that stay with me: choking down smoky-tasting milk warmed over a wood fire in order to keep my promise to Sister Luke—two cups of milk per day, no exceptions; the best kabobs imaginable, from a vendor near the Khyber Pass; all those weapons; and that man who wanted to buy me.

Back in East Pakistan, as the pregnancy progressed, I grew more nervous and realized I would have liked to have had Mama nearby. We communicated by letter only—intercontinental phone calls were almost impossible and the connections poor—and anyway, I didn't want to worry her. I knew she must be frantic with worry already. So I dealt with most of my fears alone, not wanting to alarm Harvey either. What if I couldn't make it to Dhaka when the time came to deliver? What if the plane didn't fly that day? What if things happened quickly and at night? Did I really want to give birth in a Catholic hospital? There was a large crucifix on the wall in each room; maybe they would baptize my baby against my will or if I died in childbirth. I knew this was ridiculous, but I couldn't shake the nagging fear. To be sure, there was the cantonment hospital at Kotbari. Harvey had been a patient there for a few days when he came down with a high fever after partaking, against his better judgment, of a meal with members of the Butchers' Cooperative. The army doctors treated him for malaria, as they did everyone with a high fever, and gave him cool baths. He had good care, and some military wives delivered their babies there, but we weren't convinced that it was the ideal place for me to give birth, and neither were our Bengali friends. We also knew Dr. Moheddin, a young local Comilla doctor who made a very nice impression, but he didn't have a maternity clinic.

I found comfort in the Peace Corps book locker, which our friends the volunteers kindly shared with us. Dr. Spock was there, for later, but of immediate interest was Dr. Frederick W. Goodrich Jr., an American obstetrician who introduced me to natural childbirth and to a British obstetrician, Dr. Grantly Dick Read, whom he called "the originator of natural childbirth." Dr. Dick Read had written a groundbreaking work, *Childbirth without Fear*, which inspired Dr. Goodrich's own book for Americans, *Natural Childbirth: A Manual for Expectant Parents*. I think I must have gotten hold of a copy of *Childbirth without Fear* because I distinctly remember reading a discussion of expectant mothers in Britain during the Blitz. These women inspired me. Well, I thought, if they could have babies safely in bomb shelters, surely I can manage at Kotbari! I studied Dr. Goodrich's text as carefully as anything I ever read at the university. I memorized all the natural childbirth exercises and practiced them religiously. Harvey learned his support role, too. We would be ready for anything, I vowed.

One rainy, windy day at the beginning of March, about seven months pregnant, I started to bleed, and all my worst nightmares came true. It was a Kathmandu day for the airbus. For some reason the Green Arrow wasn't running. There was nothing to do but get me to Holy Family by road. Dr. Moheddin said I had to travel flat on my back, impossible in our VW Beetle. Harvey asked the nuns at the convent school to lend us their van, which they agreed to readily and loaned us their driver as well. Dr. Moheddin came along, ready to give me a morphine injection if needed. He and Harvey improvised a stretcher and carried me to the van. And that was the last time I saw my beautiful bungalow.

I don't remember much about that trip, except that fear held me in its firm grip. *What if? What if?* Sister Luke met us at Holy Family and examined me. Perhaps I was going to have a placenta previa, a potentially very serious condition in which the placenta is located too close to the cervix; if the bleeding started up again, I would need a caesarian section immediately. Could I remain in Dhaka until the birth? Sister Luke asked. Impossible: we couldn't impose on our American friends for such a long time, and Harvey had to be at Kotbari. Then she recommended that I fly back to the United States as soon as possible. Everything looked normal; there was a tiny chance that I might be carrying twins, but it was so unlikely that we shouldn't think about it. We didn't.

The Population Council graciously bought me a seat on a PIA flight to Calcutta, and a first-class ticket on SAS flights from Calcutta to Copenhagen and from Copenhagen, via Montreal, to Chicago. We stayed a few days with our friends who worked for the Ford Foundation, and I got ready for the trip. I had no maternity clothes, but our host had a copy of *The New Yorker* from several months back, with an ad from a maternity shop. We paid a visit to a seamstress, who copied the two dresses pictured for me in a day. As we prepared to leave for the airport, a shoulder seam opened, and our friend had to sew me into the dress I had chosen for the flight. I had no maternity hose, so I flew bare-legged, wearing the comfortable Bengali sandals I had lived in since arriving. But my legs were covered with mosquito bites. Mama gasped when she saw me. I was thin, down nearly thirty pounds, thanks to Sister Luke, and I carried the baby (babies) inconspicuously.

I didn't look seven months pregnant, which was probably a good thing; I don't think the airline would have been enthusiastic about ferrying me halfway around the world, even though it was legal. But had any of us known that I was only five weeks from delivery, I suspect the whole trip would have been off. Sister Luke had given instructions that I be met at every stop along the route with a stretcher and a wheelchair and that I be taken directly to the nearest hospital should bleeding recur. Harvey came along to Calcutta and saw me onto the SAS plane. And then, on March 14, 1965, what I came to think of as the Trip from Hell commenced.

I don't remember all the stops, but I'm pretty sure we touched down in Karachi, Tehran, Beirut, Frankfurt—I had sent Stefan a telegram saying that I might need him to come to Frankfurt—Zurich, and, finally, Copenhagen. At each stop a flight attendant asked me how I felt. I hardly knew how to answer: exhausted and numb and scared. *Could you please bring me Mama?* Every half hour or so, I checked for bleeding. *All's well so far, but will I make it past the next city? Please, God, let me make it past the next city!* Every few minutes, it seemed, they served me elegant Scandinavian meals and offered wines; I was, after all, traveling first class. But what a waste! I barely touched anything, nauseated as I was, sore from internal kicking, mosquito bites itching unbearably. In Copenhagen I changed planes and flew on to Montreal and Chicago. I can still picture the Spanish businessman who sat next to me on the flight from Montreal, whose impeccable suit I ruined as I fumbled for the air-sickness bag.

I staggered off the plane in Chicago, and I imagine I had a desperate look, because I was treated very nicely by immigration and customs officers and passed through quickly. *If this wild-looking young woman is going to collapse or explode, let it be on someone else's watch*, I imagined them thinking.

Papa and Mama met me as I emerged from customs and whisked me off to Chicago Lying-In for an appointment with the obstetrician they had found for me. Dr. Harrod was large and calm, the father of five, and unflappable. The bleeding had stopped and never did recur. "You'll be fine," he said. "Expect an eight-pound boy about eleven weeks from now."

He was the first in Chicago to make that prediction but not the last. At home, Grandma looked at me from all angles and said, exuding folk wisdom, "a boy." That night, my first at home, I fell into bed, exhausted, and cried myself to sleep. What was happening to me? I missed my husband, my bungalow, the tropics. March in Chicago: raw, cold. That awful flight home. My maternity dress, which Mama had to cut me out of. And the baby kicked and kicked. In the course of the next five weeks I wondered how one small baby, with two arms and two legs, could possibly cover such a wide area, all at once.

Papa's brother Archie, our unofficial family doctor, came down from Milwaukee, looked me over, and said, "a boy, eight pounds." Mama took me to a department store, and we bought some real maternity clothes. We bought nothing for the baby; Mama and Grandma explained that it was considered bad luck to do so before the baby was born. (I think this superstition is widespread and not limited to Jews from Eastern Europe.) I spent my days reacquainting myself with American life, visiting with friends, writing aerograms to Harvey. I missed the tropics, my saris and sandals, the intense sunlight, the bright green jungle, the many varieties of bananas and mangoes, my Bengali friends, and Harvey.

Looking back, I realize, with complicated feelings, that for months at a time I didn't think about Russia much at all. Clearly, my personal self overwhelmed my professional self. Marianna the Wife and soon-to-be Mother pushed Marianna the Russian Scholar firmly out of the picture. The interlude in East Pakistan, the drama of my pregnancy and trip home, simply wiped Russia from my mind. I didn't realize it then, but I had become a junior member of a sisterhood, Women Who Work Outside the Home and Worry about It. I wasn't worried yet, but I would be, soon enough.

Passover that year began on Friday, April 16. I don't recall much about our seder, beyond the fact that it was small, quiet, and at our house, but I do remember that Nelly had arrived that day from Ohio for a short visit. Nelly was our Peace Corps nurse friend, home after finishing her tour, and I was delighted to see her, a link to Kotbari and Harvey. I woke up, however, that Saturday morning soaking wet. What an embarrassment! When I told Nelly, she smiled at me.

"Call the doctor," she advised.

"What?" I shrieked. "This couldn't be the baby, could it? It's six weeks too early! It can't be!" But I called, and Dr. Harrod told me not to worry. Sometimes the water broke early, and I might need to check into the hospital, to protect against infection. Was I having contractions? "What do contractions feel like?" I asked.

"If you have to ask, you haven't had any," he answered. "Stay in touch."

We spent a quiet day. Saturday evening we had a small second seder, just Mama, Papa, Grandma, Nelly, and me. Dr. Harrod called to find out how I was.

"Not very hungry," I said, "and I feel sort of funny."

"I'll meet you at the hospital," he replied, "just in case."

"But I'm not ready psychologically," I protested to Nelly and my parents. They laughed. I checked into the hospital at about 8 p.m., Mama with me in place of the usual husband, and I settled down to read until something happened, if anything were going to happen. My novel was one I had just bought, John Barth's *The Sot-Weed Factor*, featuring a pair of twins, I learned as I read.

Labor started at about 11 p.m., intensely, and never let up. Mama wiped my forehead with a damp cloth and cheered me on. Papa hovered in the hall and camped in the waiting room, probably working. Periodically, teams of two came into my room—medical students, interns, nurses—and placed their stethoscopes on my belly, listening for heartbeats; by now, people were beginning to take the possibility of twins seriously. I didn't know why and was too busy to care. I was barely aware of their presence, because I was working so hard, concentrating on Dr. Dick Read's natural childbirth exercises, thinking of those brave moms during the Blitz, trying to be like them.

Sometime during the night a nurse said something positive about my command of the exercises and asked where I had taken a class. No class, I explained; I taught myself from a book. My, was she startled! Throughout, we had accompaniment from a neighboring room, shrieking, rising and falling, at full volume, and in the brief interludes we heard a gentle voice reasoning with the sufferer, admonishing her: "Now, Mrs. Smith, let's not carry on so. This is *your eighth baby! You know how it goes by now!*"

Around dawn, an experienced labor nurse came in as the latest team of belly listeners finally picked up two heartbeats. She listened herself and pronounced, "There could be more than two. Be prepared!"

"You can't be serious!" I shrieked.

She nodded sagely. They wheeled me into the delivery room, where Dr. Harrod was waiting.

"Doctor," I pleaded, "I'm really exhausted. I've been working hard all night. Would you knock me out, please?"

"You're almost done," he said. "In a few minutes you'll have a good rest. Let's see what we have here."

Kate emerged first, followed three minutes later by Mary. (They were actually Choldin Baby 1 and Choldin Baby 2 at that point.) A nurse laid them on my tummy for a moment and then whisked them away into incubators. I remember feeling relieved, battered, exhausted, triumphant; then I sank into blissful sleep.

"Two girls," Dr. Harrod told my stunned mother, hovering outside the delivery room door, "and they're healthy—they don't need oxygen, but we'll keep them in intensive care until they're bigger." For the record, Kate weighed 4 pounds 6 ounces, and Mary, 3 pounds 9 ounces, for a total of 7 pounds 15 ounces, so all those eight-pound guesses were not far off; only the number of babies and the gender were wrong.

I woke up in a double room, with an Easter basket by my bed and a big holiday breakfast, with matzoh, as I had requested, to replace the Easter bun on my tray. When Papa came a little later, he told me he'd sent Harvey two telegrams, one to our bungalow and one to our friends in Dhaka, announcing the night's events. Harvey reported that some academy staff members consoled him for having daughters: "It's OK," they said. "The Prophet's first children were girls."

I stayed in the hospital for a few days, as was the custom then. Each day I had lessons on how to bathe a baby—they gave me an infant-sized doll, as I wasn't allowed to touch my daughters, and my roommate, who had just delivered her third baby, let me practice on hers. The pediatrician who had cared for Susan and me as kids, Dr. Calvin, was caring for the twins now. He explained that bottle feeding would be best, as the doctors could keep changing the formula to see what would put weight on those little bodies most quickly. I had hoped to nurse and cried when my milk came in, but I trusted Dr. Calvin and the team at Lying-In, and I didn't protest.

I understood now what Dr. Harrod had told Mama at the door to the delivery room—that my babies were at risk—but I wasn't worried: they were, after all, in the best place. I didn't allow myself to think about what might have happened had I stayed in East Pakistan: that was altogether too scary. Dr. Moheddin? The cantonment hospital? Even Holy Family didn't seem as wonderful from my current vantage point. Of course, they might have been fine, but I didn't want to consider what might have been. Better to follow my usual path: stride forward optimistically; don't look back.

The highlights of my days were my walks to the premature nursery. A nurse wheeled two Isolettes over to the window, and I watched those tiny beings, identical in every way except size. (Kate was three-quarters of a pound heavier than Mary, a significant difference when their combined weight was just under eight pounds.) I watched doctors, nurses, medical students cuddling the girls, gently moving their tiny arms and legs up and down, feeding them. As I pressed my nose against the glass, craning my neck for a better look, I experienced the first of the many ambivalent feelings that are part of parenthood. I wanted very badly to hold them. I yearned for them. But at the same time I was relieved that professionals were in charge of these precariously small beings, that I didn't have to be responsible for them yet.

I was scared, truth to tell. My experience with infants was limited to a few babysitting dates in the apartment upstairs when I was eleven—the children were always asleep, leaving me time to read—and a summer as a "mother's helper" for my older cousin, in Chicago for a few weeks with her newborn baby daughter. I don't think I actually had touched that baby more than a half-dozen times; mainly I ran errands for my cousin. And here I was, with two tiny premature infants for whom I was responsible. Help! The hospital was the right place for them, as long as they could stay there.

When I was discharged, Papa drove me to the hospital every day to visit the babies, who had to remain there until each reached five and a half pounds. It took Kate four weeks to reach that goal, so after she came home, I went back to the hospital daily to see Mary, who needed an additional week. "I'll really miss her," the nurse who discharged her told me. "She was my best eater!"

At home at last with both daughters, I thought I would adjust with no trouble at all.

What could be so hard about getting through the night with two babies? The worst was over, wasn't it? We had come so far together! I had carried them in my body, safely, from Kotbari to Chicago, and delivered them in a fine hospital. I had had some time to rest and adjust to the shock of twins. Kate had been home for a week, and we had managed nicely, Mama, Papa, and I—it wasn't easy, but I felt confident that I could do it. Now Mary was home too, and we were all together in the house on Woodlawn Avenue. Everything would be fine.

But after a single sleepless night, I capitulated. It seems that infants make lots of noises while they sleep, some of them quite alarming, and I jumped up each time I heard one. And in those rare moments when one or the other wasn't making noise, I grew nervous. Were they breathing? I had to get up and check, placing a hand on each tiny chest. And then, of course, they woke up—not together—every two to three hours, famished, and had to be fed. The bottles were in the refrigerator, in the kitchen, and had to be warmed. Our bedrooms were on the second floor.

The morning after that sleepless night as a mother of twins, Mama, Papa, and I made a battle plan. We would separate the girls at night, one sleeping with me and one with them, exchanging babies every third night. This plan worked pretty well. Papa and I each fed our charge when she woke up, hungry. (Mama slept, saving her strength for the daytime shift.) Papa and I met often, in the deep of night or as dawn approached, on the stairs, one of us going down to get a bottle, one coming up, bottle in hand. We sat in the study while we fed the girls and watched movies on television. This was my introduction to *Dr. Strangelove, or How I Learned to Love the Bomb*. I'll always identify that dark zaniness with the sweet, milky smell of baby in my arms and with the close, companionable hours with Papa.

In the mornings Papa went to the office, although I think he really wanted to stay home some days. Mama and I carried on all day, while Grandma looked on approvingly, cooing with delight. We struggled to feed the babies on a three-hour schedule, waking one if necessary. We hoped to grab short naps while they slept, but I rarely managed to do it: too much else needed to be done. I prepared formula, a big operation: we had two sterilizers, each holding eight bottles, and they got quite a workout. So did I, running up and down the stairs between nursery and kitchen dozens of times a day (and night), fetching full bottles, washing used ones, sterilizing again and again. We gave the dirty diapers (ninety, twice a week) and soiled baby clothes to a laundry service. The big, burly delivery men looked out of place in their pink and blue trucks with storks painted on the sides, each holding a bundle of joy, wrapped in a diaper, in its beak. In Chicago at that time, linen services were said to be part of mob operations, and the appearance of the drivers made this seem quite plausible to us.

Then there were the baths. I insisted on a full bath for each baby every day, cleaning the little plastic tub and changing the water between baths. I believe there was wide agreement at that time—perhaps now as well—that this was unnecessary. I think I recall that Dr. Spock, whose manual I had borrowed permanently from the Peace Corps book locker and carried home from Kotbari, and Dr. Calvin, who had been my pediatrician and was now in charge of my daughters' health, agreed that I didn't have to change the water, but I was having none of it. I carried that heavy little tub, full of soapy water, to the bathroom (on the same floor as the nursery, fortunately), washed it out in the bathtub, filled it up again, staggered back to the nursery, and started over with the second baby.

On those rare occasions when both babies slept at the same time, I wrote to Harvey and trotted to the corner to mail my letter. On mild days we took the girls for walks in their tank of a buggy, which barely fit normal sidewalks and made it through doorways only with difficulty. Family and friends stopped by to visit, small ripples in the sea of routine that was my life. I was too exhausted to be happy or unhappy: I just pumped my way through my days and nights, doing what needed to be done, and waited for Harvey to return so we could get on with our lives.

Four months later Harvey joined me, and we moved to East Lansing, Michigan, where he had his first teaching job at Michigan State University (MSU). We settled into a tiny rented house close to campus and established new routines and hired a local diaper service (blond, blue-eyed drivers, not gangster-like at all). Harvey learned how to be an assistant professor, teaching undergraduates, serving on committees, interacting with colleagues, and conducting research. I learned how to keep doing everything I had been doing before, but without help from Papa at night and Mama during the day. Harvey jumped in as best he could, but the main burden, if you can call it that, fell on me.

I put everything else on hold for a year and tried to be a perfect mother of twins. But I was twenty-three years old and completely overwhelmed; as I look back, I wonder how our little family survived the double shock of a first teaching job and twin babies, two hundred miles from our supportive family and good friends. Luckily for us, our best friends from Kotbari, my Bengali teacher and her husband and their infant son, had just arrived on campus—the husband was there to study for a PhD—and we began to build a circle of friends from Harvey's department. It was especially good to have our Bangladeshi friends nearby when we had our first exposure to Big Ten football, particularly in a year when the MSU Spartans were riding high. Our house was near the stadium, and one fall Saturday we found ourselves out in the car with two hungry babies in need of fresh diapers, unable to get home because the major street we needed to cross was blocked by police. Our friends lived in a different part of East Lansing, and we descended on them and camped out until the game was over.

We managed, barely, but by the end of our first year in East Lansing, Harvey realized that I was ready to climb the walls and convinced me that I needed to get back to Russian studies. What a hero he was! He found me a babysitter, herself a mother of twins, and then a second babysitter—a retired nursery-school teacher, no less!—to be with the girls while I sat at the East Lansing Public Library and wrote my master's paper on those Chekhov stories, the only remaining requirement for my degree.

Then, at Harvey's suggestion (and after considerable urging), I went to see Professor Arthur Adams, a historian of Russia in charge of Russian area studies at MSU. Art was delighted to meet me; indeed, he nearly jumped over his desk to welcome me. He had been waiting for someone like me to walk through his door, he said, and explained that he and Dick Chapin, director of the MSU Library, needed me desperately to be the Slavic bibliographer. I protested that while I was an avid user of libraries, I knew nothing about working in a library. No matter, Art said; Dick's people would teach me everything I needed to know. And to my amazement, they did just that. I became a Slavic librarian, working halftime because the twins were so young. In 1969 Harvey had an offer from the University of Illinois—a place with a superb library—and I was able to continue my new career in what was arguably the most dynamic and exciting Slavic library in the country. What a stroke of luck!

Looking back, I see that my year with the babies, like my time in East Pakistan, was not just a diversion. Those three years were important for my development as a Russian scholar, a library activist, and a caring human being. It was good for me to be jolted out of my trip on autopilot to a PhD; good to be immersed in a very different culture and language; good to be humanized by parenthood (Papa's concept); good to grow up a little, to be anchored by other people, and not to think only of myself. When I launched myself again, I did so onto a new path. I still loved Chekhov and the other giants of Russian literature. But now I wanted to learn about the society in which they lived and worked, and I wanted to do it as a scholar-librarian.

CHAPTER 4

LIFE IN THE LIBRARY

I loved my work from the very first morning at the MSU Library. I was given a desk in the acquisitions department, where I was surrounded by a usually genial, mostly gentle, sometimes quirky group of people among whom I was to live for the next thirty-five years, first in East Lansing and then in Urbana. The room seemed enormous to me, the walls lined with shelving stuffed with books. All the desks, and there were dozens of them, were covered with stacks of books and papers, and leaning towers of books dotted the floor between desks. Navigating was an acquired skill. It was a bright, cheerful, cluttered place. Potted plants and family photos made the atmosphere homey. There was always a low buzz of conversation and light laughter. We had frequent parties celebrating birthdays and just for the fun of it, and colleagues from various ethnic backgrounds brought wonderful dishes from their homelands. We gathered around desks and a couple of large tables, and copious amounts of food disappeared in no time at all.

As I worked with librarians around the world in later years, I realized that I could spot a librarian anywhere, although I don't really understand how. It has to do, I think, with a certain intensity and persistence, a passion for organizing information and seeking answers to difficult and esoteric questions, no matter how long the search might take. Librarians excel at crossword puzzles, and they love challenges. Wherever I go in the world, I feel at home instantly in their libraries and work spaces. I enjoy the collegiality of kindred souls, bask in the smell of their book stacks (musty from decaying paper), and find old friends among their reference books.

Acquisitions Department colleagues dealing with Western Europe told me about "blanket orders," a term that was new to me: a dealer who specialized in publications from a particular country or region would make an agreement with our library to provide books and journals to us according to a profile we built. We wouldn't need to select items title by title, a very labor-intensive process for which many libraries, including mine, had insufficient staff. (In our country Harvard was unusual at that time in using individual selectors; almost all the other academic and research libraries with serious Slavic and East European collections used blanket orders for current publications.) One of my new colleagues had heard about a dealer in Munich, Kubon & Sagner, that would set up blanket orders meeting our needs. Professor Adams made sure I met "my" faculty—the professors specializing in Slavic languages and literatures, history, political science, economics— and together we built our profiles and fine-tuned them with Kubon & Sagner, and soon the boxes were arriving steadily from Munich.

Why from Munich and Kubon & Sagner, rather than directly from Moscow, Warsaw, Budapest, and so on? Because, I learned, the book business on the other planet was nothing like ours. First of all, they didn't have a commercial book trade, as we did. All books over there were published by the state. And without "hard" currencies traded on world markets, like dollars and yen, and without open borders, they couldn't conduct a Western-style book trade. Their publishers and booksellers weren't permitted to deal directly with customers on our planet. Instead, a special agency was established in each country. In the Soviet Union it was called Mezhdunarodnaia kniga (International Book). A small number of book dealers on our planet (usually only one per country) became agents of Mezhkniga, as it was known, and its sister agencies in other countries on that planet, and those dealers could then establish their own blanket orders for books from our planet. Our libraries paid the dealers, the dealers settled up with the official agencies, and the books flowed.

My learning curve was steep. At the beginning my Michigan State University colleagues had to teach me absolutely everything about being a librarian, and they did so with grace and patience. No one seemed to resent me because I didn't have a library degree. Indeed, they welcomed me with open arms because I was there to rescue them from having to deal with publications from the Soviet Union and Eastern Europe, printed in unfamiliar languages and funny alphabets, the majority reeking of the strong, sour smell of Soviet paper, far more penetrating than that of European or American paper. (Evidently, the other planet had its own methods of milling paper.) I knew that smell from my studies, of course, but now I lived with it as a professional, and it clung to my skin and clothes. I didn't realize then how evocative that smell was, or how much symbolism I would attach to it, and how it would invade my imagination.

The faculty members in Russian and East European studies at MSU were equally kind and patient. They too were delighted to have me, because now they would no longer have to function as librarians themselves, trying to build the collections they needed to support their teaching and research while they taught and did research. I met periodically with each one to learn his or her needs and encouraged them to help me. They understood that it would take some time for me to get up to speed and put no pressure on me. The combination of Russian studies and librarianship pleased me enormously, and I was delighted with my role as liaison between my faculty and the library. I thought of myself as a scholar-librarian in the making.

When I came to Illinois in September 1969, I learned about the other channel through which books and journals flowed. When a university or other research library needed older, out-of-print material, or new scholarly items published by academic institutions on the other planet, it usually obtained them through an elaborate system of exchanges. Just as we had difficulties buying publications from them, they couldn't buy directly from us, because their libraries had very limited access to hard currencies. To get around this huge problem, we developed a barter system together, based on a rough dollar-for-dollar equivalency. Libraries on their planet had plenty of copies of their own publications, even if they didn't have hard currencies, and they could send books and magazines to us at no cost to themselves, because the state paid the freight for them. We sent items published by our university and trade presses. The university press books were free to us or provided by our universities at low cost, and we had deep discounts from trade publishers. Exchanges were a great deal for libraries on both planets during the Cold War years.

At some large libraries in the United States, including Illinois, some of these exchanges resembled blanket orders. For instance, we would build profiles of the kinds of new materials we wanted to receive from the Academy of Sciences Library in Leningrad, and we would send them requests for individual items of older material needed by American scholars—runs of certain journals and newspapers, for example. At large research libraries such as Illinois, we were building collections not just for our own faculty and students but also to serve scholars throughout the country and the rest of our planet.

For Soviet and East European libraries these exchanges were, for the most part, the only way they could obtain publications from our planet, and so they were incredibly important. Libraries on the other planet developed profiles, as we did, and made individual requests, as we did. They relied on us for all kinds of publications: scholarly and scientific materials in many fields and belles lettres, classic and modern. We made arrangements with our university and trade presses to provide what our partners asked for. Many, perhaps most, of the items we shipped went directly into *spetskhrany*—those special, closed collections—but at least they were there, in the country, and scholars who could prove their reliability and their need to consult these materials might have a chance to read them.

I've always been amazed that the thousands of boxes of books shipped both directions by hundreds of libraries on the two planets sailed beneath the radar, somehow. From time to time during the Cold War a US congressman would learn about this traffic and rumble that we were allowing valuable information to flow to the enemy, and I suppose the same fears were raised on the other planet, but the flow continued. I took real pride in being part of this system, and I know many of my colleagues did too. We groaned when endless boxes of the complete works of dictators would arrive—Albania's Enver Hoxha; Romania's Ceausescu; Marx, Engels, Lenin, Stalin, and on and on, ad infinitum—but we knew this was the price we had to pay to get the good stuff into libraries on both planets.

At Illinois I found support for what became my main goal: to provide scholars with the materials they needed, regardless of where the scholars and the materials were located. I was one of the organizers of the Summer Research Laboratory on Russia and Eastern Europe, an ingenious program, started in 1973, that attracted scholars from all over the world to our campus in the summers by giving them a place to stay and faculty privileges in our great library. In 1976 I became the first director of another innovative program, the Slavic Reference Service, which helped scholars worldwide to locate and obtain materials they needed for their research (even before the advent of the Internet).

Though only a few short years have passed, it's hard now to remember what research was like before the Internet. Scholars needed all the help they could get from people like my Slavic-librarian colleagues and me. We phoned each other at libraries around the country to check holdings. We wrote letters to colleagues outside North America. We sent telexes to librarians in the Soviet Union and Eastern Europe requesting microfilm of a run of newspapers some scholar here needed. We kept at it until we found what we were searching for. Rarely did we give up.

The Summer Research Lab and the Slavic Reference Service were based on three strengths: our rich collections, our ability and willingness to share them with scholars everywhere, and our incredibly strong team of librarians who carried out the painstaking work of locating and obtaining research materials from other libraries around the world. These two programs made our library famous, and working there made me feel proud and happy. The scholars we helped, hundreds of them, came to trust us and rely on us; they waited patiently, sometimes for years, until their ship came in. And when it did and we were able to call or write to them with the good news, the thrill was unlike anything I had ever experienced.

My colleagues at Illinois were mainly American born, but we were aided in our work by émigrés from Eastern Europe and by a large number of Soviet émigrés of the "Third Wave," most of them Jews or married to Jews, who left the Soviet Union starting in the 1960s, peaking in the 1980s and 1990s. (The "First Wave," including my grandparents, had fled anti-Semitism; the "Second Wave," less Jewish in composition, had fled Communism after the 1917 revolution; and the "Third Wave" fled anti-Semitism again.) Many Third Wavers who landed near universities sought employment there, and quite a few were drawn to libraries with Slavic collections. At Illinois, and at university and research libraries throughout North America and Western Europe, we Slavic librarians hired these émigrés to work in our libraries, regardless of their backgrounds: they knew Russian, and that was what mattered.

For me, the émigrés were also an important link to the other planet. I felt a bond with them, almost as though they were family—the Jewish cousins, nieces, and nephews from whom I had been separated when my grandparents emigrated. During my years in Champaign-Urbana I hired or worked with a number of them. A few became good friends, but as new Americans, not as Soviet citizens. Like so many new Americans, most of them wanted to fit in, to become like us, not to talk about where they came from. They worked in the Slavic Library because their English was too weak to work anywhere else, but they looked forward, not backward.

Libraries are welcoming places for people with knowledge of a foreign language, and I used to write letters on behalf of the American Library Association for people trained as librarians in the former Soviet Union who were now seeking library jobs in the United States. I studied their credentials and wrote each one a letter: "Your coursework, aside from the political courses [which usually had the names Marx and Lenin in the course titles and were completely useless substantively], is similar to the coursework in US schools of library and information science." (Or, in some cases, it was not similar, and I had to tell them that they would need additional study in the United States to qualify as a librarian.)

As much as I tried to help émigrés, it didn't always work out well, and sometimes they resented my efforts. Often their expectations far exceeded the reality: a chemist didn't want to demean himself by working at a menial job in a library. My heart went out to these people, some no longer young, who had to make new lives for themselves and their families in a new country and, worst of all, in a new language. Over the years I saw several of their children grow up to become genuine Americans, often bright and talented ones, sometimes active members of the American Jewish community. But my main focus was always on the Old Country, where they came from, and most of the émigrés didn't share my fascination with that place.

Still, my émigré colleagues were willing to talk with me about their former home, and I learned a lot about the way things worked in the Soviet Union, and about Soviet culture, from listening to and observing them. Despite their strong prejudices, they were a great resource for me when I didn't understand something or wanted to test an idea. For example, when I was working in the early 1980s on comparing American originals with their Soviet translations, I asked a couple of émigré friends to read passages, first in Russian and then in the English-language original. Without exception they were stunned and horrified by the changes that had been made and assured me that had they read the translation while still living in the Soviet Union, they never could have guessed what the original text was. When they lived in the Soviet Union and read a translation of a foreign book, they just assumed that it was accurate. They validated my work, which was so important to me.

Over the years I became a sort of roving ambassador for the world community of Slavic scholars and librarians, working mainly through the organizations that brought us together: in North America, the American Association for the Advancement of Slavic Studies, and organizations of Slavic-specialist librarians in the United Kingdom, France, and Germany. The Cold War was still on, and we could work with our colleagues on the other planet only on an individual library-to-library basis, below the radar screen, but a number of us did develop excellent relationships, mainly through the institutional exchange of materials I've described. Some of my American and European colleagues made frequent trips to the Soviet Union and Eastern Europe, and they were helpful to the whole community on our planet, sharing reports of their visits, contacts, and the latest rumors about the library world on the other planet.

I worked at the library mornings only until the girls were eight years old, when I increased to three-quarters time and started on the tenure track, eventually increasing again to full time. At the beginning I had been really worried about finding a way to combine my work and my scholarship with being a mother and a wife. Papa was a fine model, except that he had a wife who didn't work outside the home and an in-house mother-in-law to boot. What was I going to do about a wife? How would I do all the things I remember Mama and Grandma doing when I grew up: laundry, cooking, shopping for groceries, daily picking up around the house, paying bills, taking kids to the doctor, and being home with them when they were sick? Just thinking about it overwhelmed me. But we did manage, thanks to flexible academic schedules; housecleaning and babysitting help, including some sitters who were also wonderful cooks and helped out with dinners; Harvey's constant cooperation; and our amazingly self-sufficient twins. Of course, there was tension between my two lives, but it never became unbearable.

By the time I started on the tenure track, Kate and Mary were busy with after-school activities, so I stayed on campus in the afternoons, did research, and wrote articles about nineteenth-century Russian bibliographers. I was blissfully happy. The University of Illinois and the library supported my work and awarded me tenure in 1976, and that same year, at Harvey's urging, I decided to take a leave without pay for one academic year and finish my doctoral studies at the University of Chicago.

I knew I wanted to combine Russian studies with librarianship, and the Graduate Library School at the University of Chicago welcomed me and made it possible for me to do what I wanted. They gave me credit for my master's work in Slavic languages and literatures and required of me one academic year in residence, followed by comprehensive exams. My plan was to find a dissertation topic, write a proposal, and defend it, all during that academic year. In the summer I would return to Champaign-Urbana and my job, take a couple of reading courses, and work on my dissertation as I could, all while working full-time. An ambitious schedule, to be sure, but I was young and energetic; academia was the only life I knew, and everyone around me was working hard. I would manage somehow.

Starting in late September and through the first half of June, Harvey dropped me at the Greyhound bus station every Sunday afternoon and I rode to Chicago, studying and napping on the way. From the bus station I took a city bus to Hyde Park, arriving at my parents' apartment around dinnertime. Mama and Papa would be waiting, and Papa would make me an omelet. (He made delicious omelets, and I think of him whenever I make them for Harvey and me on Sunday nights.) What a strange and precious time it was! Living at home again, being cared for by my parents, packing a lunch and going off to "school" each morning. My classmates were mostly younger than me, recently out of college. We studied together, struggling through required statistics and computer courses. I was already a practicing librarian but knew little about the field outside my Slavic experience. I absorbed what seemed useful to me and stored the rest, to be used at exam time.

I stayed with my parents until Thursday or Friday afternoons, when I would return home on the train or, occasionally, with an Urbana friend in the city on business, who drove us both. At home on the weekends I cooked for Harvey and the girls. Most of the time they left my chicken dishes in the freezer and ate out or brought in pizza and watched *The Brady Bunch* or *Barney Miller* on TV. They were all happy to see me but didn't seem to be suffering unduly, a great relief to me. Mama worried about them, and I was glad to be able to reassure her.

In June I passed my comprehensive exams and prepared to defend my dissertation proposal. My topic had chosen me unexpectedly. One day in the fall of 1976, when I was back in Urbana for a few days, I bumped into my colleague, Professor Maurice Friedberg, in the library. Maurice had come to Urbana from Indiana University a few years earlier, and we had become fast friends. A Polish Jew who had survived the Holocaust in Poland—how? he never discussed it—Maurice was a specialist, among other things, on Soviet translations of Western literature and had written two marvelous books on the subject. He spoke several languages flawlessly and was renowned among colleagues far and wide, including those inside the Soviet Union, for always knowing the latest Soviet jokes.

Maurice had just come across a book on our library shelves and brought it to my attention, an ordinary-looking bibliography from the prerevolutionary period entitled *Alfavitnyi katalog sochineniiam na frantsuzskom, nemetskom i angliiskom iazykakh, zapreshchennym inostrannoiu tsenzuroiu ili dozvolennym k obrashcheniiu s iskliucheniem nekotorykh mest, s 1856 po 1 iiulia 1869 goda* (Alphabetical Catalog of Works in French, German, and English Banned by the Foreign Censorship or Permitted with the Excision of Certain Passages from 1856 through 1 July 1869).[1] The book was divided into three sections, one for each language. Each entry consisted of a good bibliographic description—author, title, place of publication, publisher, year of publication, number of pages—and beneath the entry the decision taken by the Foreign Censorship Committee. An item might be banned in its entirety; or banned "for the public," or "for doctors," or "for Protestants"; or permitted "with excisions," with the passages to be excised listed specifically.

---

1   *Alfavitnyi katalog sochineniiam na frantsuzskom, nemetskom i angliiskom iazykakh, zapreshchennym inostrannoiu tsenzuroiu ili dozvolennym k obrashcheniiu s iskliucheniem nekotorykh mest, s 1856 po 1 iiulia 1869 goda* (St. Petersburg: Tip. Ministerstva vnutrennikh del, 1870).

What did all this mean? I didn't know anything about this subject yet, but I did instantly know one thing—here, in the pages of this peculiar, slim volume, was the perfect topic for me: the censorship of foreign books in imperial Russia. Maurice knew it too, of course, and from that moment on, he was not only my friend and colleague but also my scholarly mentor.

I remember turning the pages of the alphabetical catalog, and within moments I was experiencing that mysterious and wonderful shock one gets when everything falls into place. For me, it's a quickening of all the senses: I feel a rush of adrenaline, joy, and confidence that something "right" has happened. I read French and German easily, and I'd always been interested in censorship but knew only that it existed in imperial Russia and the Soviet Union; I had no idea at all about how it actually worked. I was eager to learn about this government body called the Foreign Censorship Committee—I'd never heard of it before—and to see how it handled these materials.

A little research revealed that the committee had been established in 1828 in St. Petersburg, the imperial capital, with branches in other cities of the empire. Each office of the committee was charged with reviewing publications entering the empire. How did they operate? Who were the censors? What kinds of publications did they review, and how did they review them? What happened to works after they passed through the committee? And, at the heart of the matter for me: what, exactly, were the censors looking for?

I wrote a proposal presenting the idea of my research, the methodology I would use to carry out the research, and a review of the literature on my subject and set a date with my advisor and the dissertation committee my advisor and I had put together. The questions they asked me were reasonable, and the committee members seemed satisfied with my responses. After an hour or so, they sent me out into the hall so they could decide my fate—and there I stayed. Had they forgotten about me? After about thirty minutes of intense discomfort, I knocked timidly at the door. My committee members turned toward me distractedly. Who was this person? Then they smiled, also distractedly. ("Oh, it's you!" was implied.) "You're fine," my advisor said, matter-of-factly. "We got to talking about departmental matters and forgot you were there. Sorry!"

The next morning I headed back to Champaign to begin a new phase of my life. I had two reading courses to complete on the Urbana campus, one taught by Maurice and the other by a Russian historian, for which I would receive credit at the University of Chicago. I was back in the Slavic Library and home again as a full-time wife and mother. And whenever I could, I slipped away to my fourth-floor study to work on my dissertation, alone with my censors.

CHAPTER 5

DISSERTATION AND BOOK

I'm about to enter the stacks of the University of Illinois library in Urbana, where I'm on the faculty of the Slavic and East European Library. It's winter break 1976, and I'm going to search for two nineteenth-century German books that I found in my alphabetical catalog. The titles I'm looking for were all permitted for circulation in Russia only, with the excision of certain passages. Beneath each item are precise instructions for finding those passages: for instance, page 29, six lines from the bottom. The card catalog (remember those?) indicates that Illinois owns the two titles I'm looking for: two volumes of the thirteenth edition of the *Brockhaus Encyclopedia* and a world history.[1]

The University of Illinois library with its vast collections is an old building; the bookstacks have a basement and four floors that are divided into ten levels, so the ceilings are low. Metal staircases, rather like fire escapes, connect the levels. Row after row of metal shelves fill the space, floor to ceiling. The lights are dim. Today, as is often the case, I'm the only person in this part of the stacks.

I find my first *Brockhaus* volume, check the censors' catalog for my instructions, and open the volume to the right page. I gasp! What is that in the left column, where my excised passage should be? What happened to the print, and why is the paper so thin? I pull the second *Brockhaus* volume off the shelf, check my instructions, and open to the correct page. Another patch of thin paper, print scraped off! What's going on? Clutching both

---

1   Oskar Jäger, "Geschichte der neueren Zeit, 1517–1789," in *Brokhaus Enzyklopädie*, 13th ed. (Bielefeld: Verlag von Velhagen & Klasing, 1888).

volumes under my arm, I dash up to the tenth level, history, and find the German world history book that's on my list, open the volume, and my head spins. Under the portrait of Empress Elizabeth I (Peter the Great's daughter), thick black ink covers the caption, and what looks like scrap paper has been pasted over it. And there are four more examples in this history book, ink alone or with paper scraps pasted over.

I'm not a horror movie sort of person, but I can't help thinking that I'm not alone on the tenth level: a ghostly imperial Russian censor is stalking me, laughing silently. I grasp all three volumes under my arm, clamber down the stairs to level 5, and exit the stacks. Into the library office I dash, find my colleague in charge of collections, and tell him my story. We check records and learn that these volumes came into the library in the early years of the twentieth century, brought out of Odessa by Professor Simon Littman, who emigrated to this country and joined the University of Illinois faculty. The volumes were part of his father's personal library and had actually passed through the Odessa branch of the Foreign Censorship Committee; when I examined them more closely, I found the committee's stamp.

Thank you, Professor Littman, for allowing me to see three methods of excision: scraping print off the page with a razor, covering words with black ink, and pasting over passages with scrap paper. I learned later that applying that thick black ink was known, in the censors' jargon, as "covering over with caviar."

When I prepared my dissertation proposal, I decided to concentrate on the German section of the alphabetical catalog. After discussing the project with my University of Illinois colleague and good friend Seymour Sudman, an internationally known specialist on statistical sampling, I drew a sample of the publications listed and then examined the publications in my sample, one by one. Being an optimist, I assumed I would be able to find these items in one of the two great libraries at my disposal—Illinois and Chicago—and that any outliers could be obtained through interlibrary loan, the scholar's best friend. And I did find almost all of the three hundred or so items in my sample, so my optimism was justified.

Aside from my amazing, eye-opening experience with the Odessa books, things went smoothly, and I felt terrific, almost euphoric. What wonderful places research libraries are! How privileged I was to be working here on a project I found endlessly fascinating! The book stacks were an enchanted place, a dense forest of books, and I was a scholar-explorer embarked on a great adventure.

I must admit, though, that much of what we scholars do in the data collection and analysis phases of our work might strike others as uninspiring and, well, boring. There was no Internet yet, at least for civilians, and scholars acquired many paper cuts while thumbing through card catalogs in search of the titles we needed. We inked our fingers liberally while filling out paper forms for interlibrary loan requests. (Paper forms: imagine that!) Our backs ached from hunching over photocopy machines; by the mid-1970s civilization had advanced to the Photocopy Age, thank goodness, although scanning still lay in the future. We hoisted large, heavy bibliographies and catalogs off high shelves, poured over their tiny and often smudged print, and then strained our necks to shove them back into place.

Once in the stacks, we plodded patiently along miles of aisles between rows of shelves, often under very low ceilings; in order to make more space for the millions of books stored in these stacks, each floor of our old building in Urbana was divided into two floors, with metal stairs leading from one to another. Harper Library, the old building at the University of Chicago, was designed the same way, as were many other academic library buildings everywhere. The windows along the outside walls of the building were generally filthy—why pay to wash windows for the benefit of the books? (I should add that the windows in faculty offices were equally filthy!) Lights were few and far between and usually dim. When we found the stack unit we needed, we strained our arms and shoulders and perched precariously on little stools known as "library steps," reaching for heavy volumes on high shelves, and we breathed in considerable quantities of dust as we turned the crumbling pages of those volumes, printed on highly acidic paper. Often we sat on the floor to peruse these volumes, contorting our bodies to fit the narrow aisles. And I must mention the smell, a highly evocative odor of decaying paper familiar to scholars everywhere.

Looking for books in the stacks was a solitary enterprise. There were generally other scholars somewhere in my vicinity, to be sure, but with ten levels of stacks housing five million volumes, it was pretty likely that no one else would be in your neighborhood at the exact moment when you were there . . . so most of the time you were alone with those decaying volumes, the dust, the musty smell, the dim light. Pawing through crumbling volumes in search of precisely the correct edition; painstakingly counting lines of type on a page of an outdated encyclopedia; poring over passages in florid nineteenth-century German prose printed in gothic script: it was musty, dusty, neck-cramping work. No matter, I loved it: the dust, the dim light, the forest of metal bookshelves spilling over with ripe books, the smell, the silence.

The setting for a melodrama or a murder mystery? Such thoughts were far from my mind, but, indeed, something big was happening: this was where my first encounter with the work of the imperial Russian censors took place. I had imagined that this phase of my research would be routine, predictable, even boring, and that didn't bother me; indeed, I thought that was how academic research should be. It simply never occurred to me that I would have a real adventure in the stacks and that I was embarking on a journey to the dark heart of censorship.

I was moved by my encounter with the Odessa books and unsettled. I was surprised to find myself trembling after leaving the library office. I had just had a close encounter with a real Russian censor. True, I hadn't seen him in the flesh, but I had certainly sensed his presence on the tenth level of the book stacks, just around the corner. As I carried Professor Littman's books up to my study that day, I indulged in a bit of fantastical thinking. What if an imaginary being had taken up residence in my head? What if I now had my very own internal Russian censor?

This thought made me supremely uncomfortable, but I could see the utility of such a relationship. I was afraid of this creature, I despised him, but I needed to keep him around to help me with my research. I pictured him as a kind of minor-league dybbuk, probably a small-time functionary based in Odessa, not a bigwig working in the capital. A displaced soul who had now lodged with me. Once I discovered these volumes, I was connected to this genuine expert, this ghost in the stacks, who showed me how it was really done. I held in my hands two volumes that my censor had once handled: he hadn't handled them today or in my library stacks; he handled them with me in mind as the intended reader, but, nonetheless, here they were, in Urbana, Illinois, United States. As unlikely as it seemed, here they were, testimony to the successful mechanics of imperial Russian censorship and the incredible power of serendipity.

By the time of my Odessa adventure, I had accumulated a pile of photocopies of censored passages, and I was beginning to grasp the themes and concerns of the censors. For those two volumes I would have to search in other libraries and request photocopies, so I would be able to examine the passages that had been so artfully, and effectively, excised from my copies with thick black ink, razor, paste, and scrap paper. I also understood now, having held these censored books in my hands, that they and I were victims *together.* They had been disfigured, their pages defaced. I had been deprived of the ability and the right to read those censored passages. The whole process had suddenly come vividly to life for me.

From that moment on, with the help of my internal censor, I sat in my study and really began to think like a censor. Simultaneously, I thought like someone who had *been* censored. As I sat alone pouring over my passages and as the patterns began to emerge, I found myself understanding the censor's role. "Aha! That sentence certainly has to go!" I would find myself exclaiming. Why? Because it's disrespectful toward Russian royalty, or questions the tsar's power, or ridicules religion, or portrays Russians as what I've come to call "non-European barbarians." And at the same time I thought of the reader, perhaps an academic like myself one hundred years before me, and I felt his or her frustration and rage upon confronting these defaced pages.

Papa, Mama, and Maurice all helped enormously with my dissertation, from the time I first developed the idea. Papa had always been my discerning reader and often my gentle editor, for every paper I ever wrote, from elementary school on. He asked tough questions that sounded innocent but were rarely easy to answer. So I struggled, and sometimes chafed, but I endured because the paper was always better afterward. Whenever I saw Papa, he asked to read what I was working on, and after each of my many trips, he debriefed me, on the phone or in person. We would talk about what I had seen, what questions intrigued me, what troubled or enchanted me. He would listen intently with his anthropologist's ear, then ask questions that inevitably cast my experience in a new light. "Tell me more about this person who frustrates you every time you encounter him. Is he perhaps frightened of you? Are you approaching him in a way that makes him uncomfortable? Do people in his culture approach each other differently? Whom can you ask about this?"

Papa died in January 1995. How I've missed that editing, those debriefings! But I do hear his voice sometimes, as I sit in a crowded plane trying to figure out the meaning of something I've experienced. I strain to hear his side of the conversation; his voice is comforting, and sometimes I can intuit what he would say if he were sitting next to me.

Mama always kept her eye on my writing too and on Papa's, Susan's, and Harvey's when he joined the family. In the summer of 1965 she proofread Harvey's dissertation (sociology, University of Chicago) and Susan's (anthropology, Harvard) simultaneously. I sat at her kitchen table across from her, the newborn twins sleeping nearby, and we read pages to each other, first a chapter of Harvey's, then one of Susan's. Mama was the general, I the private: there was no doubt who was boss. As I mentioned earlier, no one in the family ever got away with sloppy writing or speech. Even on her deathbed, nearly comatose, she roused herself to correct the petty grammatical crimes committed by family members gathered around her. Kate and Mary spoke of her affectionately as "the grammar police," and her title has passed to me. I try to be worthy of her, but from time to time I hear her reproving whisper.

Maurice Friedberg was another invaluable reader, editor, and advisor for me. Although he was a professor at the University of Illinois, he was invited to sit on my dissertation committee at the University of Chicago. No Chicago faculty member at the time possessed sufficient knowledge of imperial Russian censorship, so Maurice worked with me as I wrote. He also directed a reading course for me and drove up to Chicago with Harvey and me for my oral dissertation defense, in the spring of 1979, dissolving the tedium of that two-and-a-half-hour ride through corn and soybean fields with a nonstop flow of Soviet jokes. The really good Soviet joke is a delightful species of humor: many-layered and richly pungent, with just a soupçon of bitterness. One of my favorites was one I heard from Papa, years before I met Maurice.

Q: What happens when International Socialism comes to the
    Sahara Desert?
A: For fifty years, nothing; then, a severe shortage of sand.

Dissertation defenses are not at all amusing, at least for the defendant. I've sat as a professor on the other side of the table for a number of dissertation committees, and now and then I've been amused, but my main emotion is empathy for the candidate; oral exams are terrifying, and there you sit, tense and scared to death, facing your committee.

Before the master's exam in Russian literature, we were given a reading list with what seemed like hundreds of titles, all of which we read doggedly, driven by fear, to prepare for the one question that we might have to answer in an essay. When you see the actual questions, you instinctively flinch and then try not to show it in case a fellow student sees you and thinks you are weak. But at least you're on your own and have time to think about your answers, to strategize, to fudge, to write petite masterpieces of evasive answers.

At the oral examination for my master's degree, the first questioner, a linguist with a strong Polish accent, invited me to name all the Slavic languages. I froze and couldn't think of a single one, not even Russian. I'd memorized them all, repeated them dozens of times, and now they were all gone. Another professor—blessings upon him!—prompted me. "Russian," he said kindly; "Polish" . . . and nodded in a friendly way. Out they spilled, all of them, and from then on I was all right.

Bad as the master's orals may have been, they are nothing compared with the doctoral ordeal. By that point you would now have been a student in the department for some years, with the knowledge that some of the professors on your committee are less than thrilled by your topic and presentation. Still others won't have expressed any interest in you at all and probably haven't read your manuscript. Moreover, some of them have doubtless been fighting with each other for decades over conflicting approaches to the field, and they may well hate each other. Dissertation defenses are open, and other faculty members and doctoral students may come to witness this rite of passage. The dissertation defense room is the Coliseum, you are the gladiator, the masses are eager for entertainment, and the lions look hungrily at you.

Usually the proceedings commence with a statement in which you attempt to briefly summarize your dissertation. You have poured your heart into preparing this statement; you've rehearsed it, torn it apart and rewritten it, rehearsed it again, discarded it, started over, prepared exhibits to illustrate your points, discarded them, and prepared new ones. You've worried about what to wear and wondered whether your voice would crack. Should I eat a meal before the defense? You've found yourself thinking: my *last* meal, perhaps?

Maurice asked the first question. I remember it clearly: "Have you got anything good to say about censorship?" This gave me a chance to describe some of the techniques Russian writers used to evade the censors, such as writing in so-called Aesopian language (a writer is really writing about contemporary Russia, but the story is set in ancient Greece). It was fun to talk about this, and I relaxed, as Maurice knew I would. After two hours I had responded to all the questions, friendly and hostile; accepted the suggestions for improvements with all the grace I could muster; argued gently on a few points. It's best of all if you can manage to get your committee members arguing among themselves, leaving you alone for a few blessed moments.

Finally, my defense was over. Except for the verdict, that is. I left the room and paced up and down the hall while the jury, my committee, deliberated. What will happen this time? History doesn't repeat itself, we're told. Someone came out of the room and ushered me in: I had passed! Receiving the congratulations of my committee and what changes I needed to make, I took Maurice off to the University of Chicago's faculty club for dinner with Harvey and my parents. The Quadrangle Club has been an important locale for me all my life: I had piano recitals there, birthday parties, family dinners with out-of-town friends, festive meals after other graduations, lunches with professors and colleagues, Lab School and college reunions, and memorial services for longtime family friends. The ambiance is gracious, the food not wonderful but not bad, either, the memories rich: I am at home there, as I am everywhere on the campus. A good place to celebrate.

Many colleagues have told me that they plodded through their dissertations, bored and impatient to be done with this distasteful but necessary exercise, and that at the end they were delighted to walk away from the topic. But this was certainly not my experience: I feel as passionate about imperial Russian censorship today as I did in 1979, when I completed the dissertation and received my degree, marching up the aisle in Rockefeller Chapel wearing Papa's doctoral hood.

Graduation Day, August 31, 1979, was a real triumph for me. Somehow I'd managed to survive three years of leading a triple life: professor and librarian at one university, doctoral student at another, wife and mother. Kate and Mary gave me a mug—much loved for years, until it broke, with "Dr. Mom" engraved on it. Harvey gave me a new watch, I suppose because he knew how important time management was to me. Papa's hood, which he placed over my head and arranged on my maroon gown, carefully so as not to disturb the black velvet beret, was an incredible and unexpected gift, presented to me when I ordered my cap and gown. I shouldn't have been too surprised; my parents bought academic regalia for my sister and me and our husbands when we all received our doctorates.

"But what about you, Papa?" I cried out when he gave it to me a few weeks earlier. "You'll be marching too when I get my degree. What hood will you wear?"

But I didn't need to worry: he had decided to wear one of his honorary doctoral hoods, so we both marched, properly attired, he with the faculty and I with the doctoral candidates, and he watched President Hannah Gray welcome me into "the ancient and honorable company of scholars."

Papa always marched when any of us got a degree. Kate and Mary graduated from the University of Chicago in 1986, and the Alumni Association planned a three-generation family photo shoot after the ceremony, starring Papa and Harvey's mother, Harvey and me, and the twins. The only problem was that Papa had disappeared. This was frustrating but not surprising: he was known for impatiently dashing off without warning and often in the wrong direction, a behavior that I either inherited or learned from him. We located him finally (not so easy in that pre–cell phone age) at home, where he had gone to wait for word from us, and the photographer had to shoot us without him. But in the next few days the staff of the Alumni Association magazine remedied the situation by pasting another photo of Papa into that group photo. Unless you knew the story, you would never guess that he had not been standing with us.

This story, which the family always repeated fondly, took on special resonance for me twenty years later when I encountered David King's superb 1997 book of photographs, *The Commissar Vanishes: The Falsification of*

Photographs and Art in Stalin's Russia.[2] In our case no commissar was airbrushed out after falling from favor, only to meet his fate in a cellar or the gulag; rather, an impatient professor was inserted into the photograph in order to be reunited with his family!

In my world, when you finished your dissertation, you began immediately to turn it into a book. Papa, Maurice, and Harvey all advised me how to do this: strip away the stiffness of language, the corset of footnotes, the uptightness of the dissertation, and let the story flow. Not long after I was awarded my doctorate, I sat in my fourth-floor study again and tried to let go. It wasn't so easy! But I had lots of encouragement from my trio of editors. Encouragement, too, came from my neighbor on the other side of the floor-to-ceiling bookcases that separated my fourth-floor study from his. The neighbor was Jack Stillinger, a well-known specialist on English romantic literature and editor of the works of John Keats. Jack knew what I was going through. Perhaps he sympathized with me because Keats had had such a bad time with reviews, and Jack knew that once I finished, I would have to submit the manuscript to some publisher. He also knew I was fragile, as all authors of first books are, and would be at the mercy of reviewers, who can be brutal.

Jack had a dry sense of humor. One hot summer day when we were the only people slogging away on the fourth floor, two students walked by, laughing and talking, unaware of us. Jack called out to them: "Hey, would you please lower your voices? We're writing a couple of books in here!" Jack doesn't remember this at all, but I'll never forget it: if someone like Jack can say casually that I was writing a book, then I had to really be writing a book that would be published, like Jack's books!

I sent my manuscript to a university press and received three reviews, two good and one devastating. (Jack must have known this would happen.) I was crushed and panicky, yet I was no novice: I'd had negative reviews before, on articles submitted to scholarly journals. Sometimes I revised the piece; other times I submitted the article to a different journal, and it had always worked out in the end. But this was different; this was staggering. Did I survive the dissertation only to be defeated by the book? I had worked

---

2   David King, *The Commissar Vanishes: The Falsification of Photographs and Art in Stalin's Russia* (New York: Henry Holt and Company, 1997).

so hard, up in that lonely, dusty study, with only Jack for company. I had struggled with every word. In my view my prose, of course, was deathless: not a syllable should be changed. Was I to surrender ignominiously to my fate? Admit defeat? Was there to be no book after all?

I phoned Maurice, and Harvey and I went right over to his house. Barbara, his wife, offered tea, and we sat at the kitchen table while Maurice read the negative review. He thought about it for a few moments, then suggested a way to reorganize the book in a way that was not too difficult and well within my reach. When I got home, I called Papa, who agreed with the strategy, as did Harvey. Mary and Kate were in their final stretch at University High School in Urbana and paid scant attention to my agony: why should they? They were working very hard on their senior English project, an all-important debate in the spring. Their teacher was demanding, and they loved her; they were willing to do almost anything for her. They were also devoted to the girls' basketball team, of which they were founding members, and they adored their coach, a young woman who commanded their loyalty no less than the English teacher did.

Mary and Kate and their flurry of activities provided me with relief from my new ordeal in the fourth-floor study, to which I retreated whenever I could, to implement the new plan for my book. Harvey and I followed the progress of their preparation for the debate, but the major source of relief for all of us was their basketball games, all of which we attended, dutifully but also with pleasure. Neither of us was athletic, yet Mary and Kate had been athletes since they learned to walk. I often told them that had I not seen them born, I would be certain that Lying-In Hospital had mixed them up with some other set of twins. They were not tall, but they were muscular, well coordinated, and passionate about the game.

Uni High is a small school, and their team played other small schools, so for away games we drove through the frigid, snowy countryside of east central Illinois to tiny towns where the locals were crazy about basketball. The girls against whom they played were twice the size of the Uni girls and much more skilled at the game, and some of the coaches were mean and merciless, or so it seemed. The scores of those games were shocking: 100-2, even 112-0. We suffered as the local players, following their coaches' instructions, subjected our exhausted daughters and their teammates to the indignity of a full-court press, over and over again. Mary threw herself heroically at oncoming opponents who towered over her: she perfected this move while her parents cringed. But the Uni girls needed our support, so we subjected ourselves to this parental torture every week or two.

Meanwhile, I spent every spare minute on the fourth floor, rewriting the manuscript. To my surprise, it fell together fairly easily, and the words flowed nicely. It turned out that my prose wasn't so deathless after all; I could revise without tears, and new prose came to me relatively painlessly. This period of rewriting was actually pleasant, and the new version of my book was much better than the old one: I knew it. Maurice, Papa, Harvey all read it and approved. I sent it off to another university press, and in due course I received good reviews. I agreed to the minor revisions recommended by the readers, and there I was, with a publisher! I'd now completed another academic rite of passage: First Book.

CHAPTER 6

MY SOVIET CENSOR

Once I knew that *Fence around the Empire* would be published,[1] I settled happily back into my library work. But in the early 1980s, I found myself thinking very often about a conversation I'd had years ago with a colleague, a Russian historian visiting from another institution during our Summer Research Lab. He had asked my opinion about imperial versus Soviet censorship: did I think they were two completely different phenomena? No, I responded promptly; the Soviet grew out of the imperial. They shared roots, but Soviet censorship was broader and deeper than the imperial version.

But after having spent hundreds of hours poring over the work of imperial censors, the themes that drove them, and the techniques they used, I realized I wasn't so sure that the shared roots were as important as I had initially claimed. I'd begun to read émigrés' accounts of experiences with Soviet censorship, as well as the few works that I could find by Western scholars. I reread a slim red book that Maurice had introduced me to in graduate school: *The Soviet Censorship*,[2] an edited transcript of a symposium held in the United Kingdom in 1967. Most of the participants were Soviet émigrés—novelists, poets, journalists, critics, a musician/composer—plus a few Western scholars who asked good questions.

For example, Albert Todd (Queens College, New York), asked, "Do people get into hot water if an article they wrote or recommended is suddenly

---

1   Marianna Tax Choldin, *A Fence around the Empire: Russian Censorship of Western Ideas under the Tsars* (Durham, NC: Duke University Press, 1985).
2   Martin Dewhirst and Robert Farrell, eds., *The Soviet Censorship* (Metuchen, NJ: Scarecrow Press, 1973).

regarded as objectionable at a late stage in the process of publication?" "Yes, they do," responded Leonid Finkelstein, a journalist before emigrating, and gave details (p. 70). And from David Anin (author, editor, commentator), "Do you find that stagnation in music is greater than in other forms of art, such as literature?" "Far greater," answered Michael Goldstein, violinist and composer, "because the censorship of music is even more ruthless" (p. 103), and he explained why.

What the émigrés had to say about freedom of expression on the other planet was riveting, searing, especially after my recent experience with imperial censorship, which now struck me as very different from, and much milder than, its Soviet successor. I couldn't get some of the émigrés' stories out of my mind. Here, for example, is the novelist Anatoly Kuznetsov on self-censorship:

> When I was still a "Soviet writer," I once experienced the great pleasure of writing without an inner censor, but it required a tremendous effort to cast off my chains and completely free myself. . . . I would bolt the door in the evenings and make absolutely certain that no one could see or hear me—just like the hero in Orwell's *1984*. Then I would suddenly allow myself to write everything I wanted to. I produced something so unorthodox and so "seditious" that I immediately buried it in the ground, because they used to search my apartment when I was away. I consider what I wrote at that time to be the best of anything I have ever written. But it was so extraordinary, so insolent, that to this very day I have not dared to show it even to my closest friends. In any case, this was a feast, an artist's spiritual feast. I do not know whether I will ever succeed in doing this again, but it was utter bliss. It pays to go on living for the sake of such moments.[3]

I hadn't thought a great deal about self-censorship. I knew it existed and that everyone, everywhere, practiced it to some extent. But Kuznetsov's experience struck me as extreme and frightening. From the time I first heard the term "self-censorship," sometime early in my dissertation research,

---

3   Dewhirst and Farrell, *Soviet Censorship*, 26.

I thought a great deal about what people have to inflict upon themselves when they live under censorship. Of course, self-censorship has always existed, in Russia and everywhere: we all censor ourselves, for a variety of reasons, some small and some enormous. Perhaps you are a teenager writing a paper for English class and you don't want your teacher and classmates to know what you are really thinking about. Maybe you are a woman in the nineteenth century, when women aren't supposed to publish novels, so you call yourself George Sand or George Eliot. And what about all the women who never managed to publish novels that lived inside them? What, I found myself thinking, about my grandmother, who buried her knowledge of the Russian language deep within herself? Self-censorship ranges from the slight and even, one might say, civilized to the enormous and barbaric.

But self-censorship takes on a particular poignancy in Soviet conditions, unlike anything in my own American experience. I was aware that intellectuals, artists, and scientists in our country had suffered during the McCarthy era, that some had been blacklisted and couldn't disseminate their work. I didn't minimize the importance of that wretched period in our country's history. Certainly many of our best and brightest, even if not on the blacklist, must have practiced self-censorship.

But rereading the red book from cover to cover made me realize that the Soviet leadership had invented something new and terrifying and that the atmosphere in which Soviet citizens lived and worked was comparable to ours only in superficial ways. With us, the rule of law underlay our national identity, and it reasserted itself eventually; the McCarthy era was an aberration, a bad dream. On the other planet there was no rule of law underlying a well-established national identity. As far as intellectual freedom was concerned, it seemed to me that Soviet citizens were living in a perpetual bad dream.

Everything about Soviet censorship frightened me, a Cold War kid. Although imperial censorship had come and gone, Soviet censorship was very much present. Imperial censorship had been European, familiar even to Americans with its concerns about sex and blasphemy. Covering with caviar, pasting scrap paper over words—these things seemed quaint, somehow: not nice and not desirable but certainly not fatal. Soviet censorship, on the other hand, had a really hard edge: barbed wire, gun towers, and the gulag. I had read Khrushchev's "secret speech" of 1956 when I was in college. By the early 1980s, twenty-five years later, I'd learned quite a bit about the crimes of Stalin, and I knew that scholars, scientists, writers, artists, composers, librarians, and all kinds of ordinary citizens were subject to this new kind of censorship, one that compelled me to further study.

When I began to study Soviet censorship in earnest, I realized that I hadn't been completely wrong when I told my colleague that this system shared roots with its imperial predecessor: although the context was utterly different, the themes and techniques were remarkably similar to those I had discovered in imperial censorship. Writers were not permitted to criticize party leaders or the party itself, nor could they write positively about religion or portray citizens of the Soviet Union as "non-European barbarians."

But the worst of it, from my point of view, was the change in the dimensions of censorship, the culture of censorship that now permeated simply everything in Soviet society and did so in a diabolically clever way. The authorities, beginning with Lenin himself, had declared that there was no censorship in the Soviet Union. Censorship, they asserted, was a bourgeois phenomenon found in countries of the decadent West. The censorship they introduced was controlled from the very top—the Central Committee of the Communist Party of the Soviet Union—and was enforced by the KGB, through personnel at every level of every social, cultural, and educational institution in the country.

This censorship, which did not exist officially, permeated everything and everybody. Each writer, painter, composer, and scientist knew what he or she must not write or paint or compose or study. But in addition— and this was new—these Soviet citizens knew what they must create or study if they wanted to succeed in their professions and, indeed, if they wanted to remain out of prison, out of the gulag, and simply alive. The better I came to know it, the more I realized that I needed a new term to describe this phenomenon, as the word "censorship" implied such a different phenomenon. So in 1990, while preparing a lecture to be delivered at the Library of Congress, I came up with the word "omnicensorship"— everywhere-censorship—and I've held onto this term ever since. In fact, Russian scholars began using the term (*vsetsenzura*), and it entered into their scholarly vocabulary.

How did these Soviet omnicensors do their work, I asked myself? Was it perhaps in the translation process that Soviet censorship was carried out? Conditions in Russia and the rest of the Soviet empire had changed radically. The borders now were closed for both people and printed matter: no more traveling to Europe to study and tour or importing foreign publications for libraries, bookstores, or individuals. Now, to the extent that most Soviet citizens had access to foreign publications, it was access made available only through Soviet-made translations. In imperial times, an unacceptable word, phrase, paragraph, or chapter was inked out and razored off the page or pasted over with scrap paper, and the reader knew instantly that something had happened. But in censorship by translation, the technique was much more sophisticated: no visible, palpable evidence remained that changes had been made.

Examining excised passages had been fruitful for me in studying the imperial period. Maybe, I thought, if I were to figure out a way to study Soviet translations of Western works, I could learn what the Soviet censors were up to. So, in 1983 I began a new research project, again with the advice of Maurice Friedberg, who had written two important books on Soviet treatment of belles lettres. *Russian Classics in Soviet Jackets* showed how the Soviet authorities treated the Russian classics, part of their own national heritage and the most popular literature among Soviet readers. The second book, *Decade of Euphoria: Western Literature in Post-Stalin Russia, 1954–64*, examined the treatment of foreign belles lettres, also much coveted by Soviet readers.[4] In each case, the authorities handled these publications with the greatest of caution as guilty-until-proven-innocent potential bearers of anti-Soviet ideology. Foreign belles lettres were the literary Ebola virus of their day and had to be handled accordingly.

In order to learn what the authorities were after, in the absence of official guides but with advice from Maurice Friedberg, I again devised an immensely labor-intensive research procedure that turned out to yield lots of fruit. What was I looking for? I wanted to see whether the translators and publishers had actually changed the books and, if so, the nature of the

---

4   Maurice Friedberg, *Russian Classics in Soviet Jackets* (New York: Columbia University Press, 1962); Friedberg, *A Decade of Euphoria: Western Literature in Post-Stalin Russia, 1954–64* (Bloomington: Indiana University Press, 1977).

change. I compared Soviet-made translations with foreign books from Great Britain, the United States, and elsewhere, focusing on six nonfiction works in English and in translation. When I looked at Senator J. William Fulbright's *The Arrogance of Power* and Studs Terkel's *Working*,[5] the familiar censorship themes and patterns immediately jumped off the page. Forbidden were criticism of party leaders or the Communist system; blasphemy against Soviet icons and heroes of the revolution such as Lenin or Stalin; indecency; and my favorite, portrayals of Soviets as non-European barbarians.

These translations also revealed to me the Soviet technique for excising passages: the Russian translations omitted anti-Soviet material. And not only did the censors or editors *omit* but also they *rewrote*, so that Senator Fulbright and Studs Turkel, despite their distinctive literary styles, sounded exactly like a Soviet writer would sound. Censorship via translation was invisible and very effective.

In 1983 I showed the retired Senator Fulbright the Soviet translation of *The Arrogance of Power*, with an exhibit of passages and their side-by-side translations. In one, Fulbright describes Cuba's regime as a "communist dictatorship," but the Russian translation calls it "communist leadership." In a passage explaining why the United States fought in Korea, Fulbright writes, "to defend South Korea against the Russian-inspired aggression of North Korea," explaining American intervention as "justified and necessary." In the Russian translation, however, the entire passage is cut. Senator Fulbright was fascinated and horrified by what I showed him, and he kept Harvey and me in his office for more than two hours. Great fun for Harvey and me!

Not so with Studs Terkel. When asked whether he would like to see what the Soviets had done to *Working*, he abruptly declined, terminating the conversation. Terkel was popular in Russia, and I think he liked that; I also think he wrote me off as a Cold Warrior. In fact the Soviet translator and editor made hundreds of changes to *Working*, drastically abridging the book by deleting 97 out of 133 interviews and retaining primarily interviews

---

5 J. William Fulbright, *The Arrogance of Power* (New York: Random House, 1966), translated as *Samonadeiannost' sily* (Moscow: Mezhdunarodnye otnosheniia, 1967); Studs Terkel, *Working: People Talk about What They Do All Day and How They Feel about What They Do* (New York: Pantheon Books, 1972, 1974), translated as *Rabota: Liudi rasskazyvaiut o svoei kazhdodnevnoi rabote i o tom, kak oni k etoi rabote otnosiatsia* (Moscow: Progress, 1978).

with unhappy workers. They discarded Terkel's introduction and added a new preface that referred to American workers as "dissatisfied, exhausted, joyless people." The original *Working* is a gem, but it was painful to read the Soviet edition.

Most Soviet censorship was invisible, as in the Fulbright and Terkel examples, but some examples of old-style, visible censorship in the age of omnicensorship did exist, though difficult to find. Picture a page in a 1949 volume of one of the national bibliographies.[6] There is a blacked-out name, one Ivanov (a very common Russian name), who had apparently published a book and then fallen out of favor. His book was no doubt pulped or sent to the *spetskhran*, the special closed collection in major libraries where books went to die. In those dark days of 1949, Ivanov himself may have been sent to the gulag or executed in a cellar. I don't know anything about this Ivanov or his book; only his surname can be seen under the ink. He is an anonymous victim.

A wonderful example that illustrates the turmoil that ensued after Stalin's death is from volume 5 of the *Bol'shaia sovetskaia entiklopediia* (Large Soviet Encyclopedia),[7] second edition, which went to press in September 1950, while Stalin still lived. There is a portrait of Lavrenty Beria, one of Stalin's most powerful henchmen and a truly evil man, with blood all over his hands. As soon as Stalin died in March 1953, his associates began to scramble for power; Beria was arrested and executed in December of that year. The article on Beria and a full-page portrait of him in the encyclopedia were undoubtedly an embarrassment to the party, so the Soviet publisher sent subscribers, including libraries around the world, a notice, in Russian, recommending that they remove the Beria article and portrait. Included in the mailing were replacement pages with text and a page of photos of the Bering Sea, alphabetically correct, to tip into the binding, with helpful directions: "The designated pages can be cut out with scissors or razor blade, preserving the inner edge, to which the new pages can be attached" (translation my own).

---

6   *Ezhegodnik knigi SSSR 1949* (USSR Book Annual 1949) (Moscow: Vsesoiuznaia knizhnaia palata, 1950), 910.
7   *Bol'shaia sovetskaia entsiklopediia*, 2nd ed., vols. 5, 12 (Moscow: Izdatel'stvo BSE, 1950–57).

The Urbana and University of Chicago libraries had received volume 5 on subscription. All of us subscribers outside the Soviet Union also received the instructions and replacement material. But while Soviet librarians were razoring and pasting because they were required to, we retained Beria in the volume, along with the replacement pages and the instructions.

In this same edition of the *Large Soviet Encyclopedia*, volume 16, is a sad entry, just twelve lines long, "*Zelenaia liagushka*" ("Green Frog"). The frog has a proper-sounding species name, in Latin, *Rana esculenta*. The story behind this innocent little frog was relayed to me by a colleague. Volume 16 was in galleys, ready to go to the printer. The twelve-line article originally in this space was devoted to a man named Zelenin, who fell from favor. The entry had to be scrapped. The editors must have been in a state of panic. What to do? Someone had a brilliant idea: invent a new species, the *zelenaia liagushka*, and describe it in twelve lines. And there is the green frog, in poor Zelenin's space, for all time.

An additional form of Soviet censorship involved airbrushing. Four pictures from David King's book of photographs tell it all: Stalin plus three comrades, two comrades, one comrade—and Stalin alone.[8]

Additionally, in the early 1980s I came across two luscious examples of censorship by translation. Both were for me a rare opportunity to see how the process actually worked, and the first was unusual due to its appearance in censored English, not in Russian translation. Published by Longman, it was a British manual of style popular worldwide for students whose native language is not English.[9] Just a few years before Gorbachev introduced glasnost and perestroika ("openness" and "economic reform"), an editor in London showed me the original texts and the changes that were to be made for the Soviet edition. "He is very unchristian" becomes "He is very unscientific." (Soviet readers don't need to hear about religion.) "The prisoner is escaped" becomes "The guest is departed." (Soviet readers don't need to hear about prisoners escaping.) "The two blue cars belong to me" becomes "The two blue cars belong to the firm." (Soviet readers don't need to hear about private ownership of cars.) Christmas becomes New Year's, Good Friday

---

8 King, *The Commissar Vanishes*, pp. 104–107.
9 Randolph Quirk and Sidney Greenbaum, *A University Grammar of English* (London: Longman, 1973).

becomes Boxing Day, Passover becomes Memorial Day. (Soviet readers don't need to hear about religious holidays.) And my personal favorite: "Nobody contributed more to the understanding of dreams than Freud" to "Nobody contributed more to the organization of the Tourist Bureau than Freud." (Psychoanalysis and its guru were absolutely banned in the Soviet Union.)

In another example of censorship through translation, a Soviet sports publisher, right before the Soviet Union fell, negotiated with Random House to bring out a Russian translation of Muhammad Ali's autobiography, *The Greatest: My Own Story.*[10] Robert Bernstein, then president of Random House, gave me access to their project files, and there I found a goldmine: an annotated copy of *The Greatest*, complete with proposed changes. These included eliminating references to Ali's fees, all profanities, and any mention of Islam and Ali's religious conversion. Bernstein, Ali himself, and his editor at Random House, who happened to be Toni Morrison, declined, and the deal fell through. The story was that when Ali was told about these proposed changes, he had "hit the roof," which must have been a sight to see. *The Greatest* remained unpublished in the Soviet Union.

As I sat alone in my study and worked on Western texts and their Soviet translations, my inner omnicensor woke up, stretched, yawned, and got ready to go to work. He taught me to think like a Soviet censor. At the same time, I found myself increasingly aware of what it must be like to be a Soviet reader, a victim of omnicensorship. My feelings were more complex and more intense than they had been in the mid-1970s, when I realized that I was identifying with both imperial censors and with victims of their censorship.

In the 1980s, when I began my project of comparing original texts with their Soviet translations, my feelings were more complex; finding that I could predict the manuscript changes that would be made caused me to squirm. But my predominant feelings were anger and disgust. How could the system distort Senator Fulbright's book and still pass it off as his? How could people be so dishonest? At least nineteenth-century Russian readers could see the caviar and guess what was under it; omnicensorship was completely invisible, and it was often impossible to read between the lines, a skill in which Soviet readers excelled. I remained haunted by the Soviet

---

10   Muhammad Ali, with Richard Durham, *The Greatest: My Own Story* (New York: Random House, 1975).

caviar covering Ivanov's name: this man and his book, both doomed. Humorous moments abound—Russian royalty can't have lovers, and Freud contributes to the "Tourist Bureau"—but overall, it's a grim business.

In the course of my dissertation research, I'd learned quite a bit about the imperial censors. Because the practice was open and acknowledged during that period, it wasn't difficult to find out who the censors were, even without access to closed archives; there were plenty of published sources for me to consult. More recently, Russian scholars have taken up this topic and have begun publishing more identities of the imperial censors. Probably the most illustrious imperial censor of Russian-language works was the novelist Ivan Goncharov. And prominent among the imperial censors of Western publications were three of Russia's greatest poets: Fedor Tiutchev, Apollon Maikov, and Iakov Polonskii. The poet-censors amazed me until I realized what a wonderful opportunity it was for these men of letters to have access to all the latest Western literature. No wonder they agreed to take on this responsibility!

No literary giants, however, have emerged among Soviet censors, at least to my knowledge. When I was doing my research, in the 1980s and early 1990s, very little information was available about the identities of the Soviet censors. The subject was top secret; no one, not even individuals who had been involved directly in one piece of it, understood how this "nonexistent" censorship worked in the broadest sense. I imagined thousands of individuals all over that immense country, each one writing (or painting, composing, carrying out scientific experiments), then reviewing, translating, editing, then finally reporting to his or her superior, who delivered it to the relevant political boss. I imagined a vast invisible network with many small nodes and larger nodes, the central node in the Kremlin. It's unlikely that not a single writer, artist, composer, or scholar ever got his or her hands dirty through censoring the work of colleagues. Of course, there must have been such cases; the dirty work can't have been left entirely to bureaucrats. We'll likely learn more as future memoirs and scholarly papers are published.

Meanwhile, I was sitting in my study and grappling seriously with my own internal Soviet censor, whose presence had become more and more evident. He had replaced his imperial Russian colleague, or perhaps the first had morphed into the second. I had been mildly afraid of the first guy when

I imagined encountering him in the Urbana book stacks, but this new ghost or figment of my imagination really upset me, and I found myself growing more agitated as I lived with him.

The hours spent in my study trying to think like a Soviet censor, prompted always by my internal guy, were the hardest I can remember in my professional life. Doing this work made me feel dirty, something I had never experienced before and hope never to experience again. And then I took off my censor's hat, as I had done a decade earlier when dealing with imperial censorship, and thought of the hundreds of millions of victims of this system, not only in the Soviet Union but also in all the countries in Eastern and Central Europe—countries that received the Soviet gift of censorship they could not refuse. I thought too about other countries that weren't part of the Soviet empire—China, Cuba, North Korea—all of which had accepted the gift of omnicensorship eagerly and implemented it enthusiastically.

Thinking about all these victims made me deeply sad and angry. I hadn't imagined that my research would be so stressful, dirty, or emotional. I yearned to make things better, or at least to see things get better, but I felt powerless. I'd written my dissertation about imperial censorship and then published it as a book, but how would that help the victims of Soviet censorship? They weren't even allowed to learn about their own censorship history, let alone cope with omnicensorship.

My sadness and anger, and my determination to help Soviet victims of censorship if I could, were fueled by what I had witnessed while researching and traveling in the Soviet Union. Self-censorship was just one disturbing aspect. Censorship, I had learned, could foster an intense physical love of books that to us might seem excessive. In the late 1980s, during the early days of perestroika and glasnost, I interviewed a number of American, British, and German publishers who bought and sold book rights to the Soviets. One publisher relayed an episode at the Moscow International Book Fair, where Western publishers came to exhibit their wares and Soviet citizens lucky enough to be admitted came to gaze on forbidden fruits.

"I'll never forget the man at an art publisher's booth who came every day for ten days, each day examining a different book," he said. "He would hold the book for one to three hours, studying and stroking it. On the last day of the fair, the publisher's representative took him into the booth. 'You've worked this booth harder than I have,' he said. 'Please choose one book as a present.' The man's eyes filled with tears. He was a professor of fine arts at a university, he explained, and he loved books."[11]

Most of us on our planet don't have this kind of physical, passionate relationship with books. Some ardent bibliophiles, obsessed antiquarians, perhaps, but your average professor of fine arts has no need for this kind of intensity. He can handle books anytime he wants to, take them home from the library, or buy them at a bookstore or from Amazon.com.

This intense attachment to the physical object, however, is not always a high intellectual pursuit. In 1988, during glasnost, someone told me a poignant story that had apparently been published in a Moscow newspaper. The story describes a man's persistent and time-consuming efforts to extract from the Lenin Library *spetskhran The Guinness Book of World Records*. He finally succeeds and holds in his hands five or six annual volumes; he is content to simply turn the pages, since he does not read English.

These incidents, and hundreds of others in the Soviet sphere with benighted governments, break my heart. And while colleagues who possess benign attitudes toward the Soviet Union are able to find aspects of Soviet life praiseworthy or worthy of being emulated, I am not; omnicensorship trumps those bright spots, and I can find nothing admirable about it. I cannot forgive the state that made Anatoly Kuznetsov bury his manuscript, that brought the professor of fine arts to tears over art books he could not have, that made a man wage such a battle to hold in his hands *The Guinness Book of World Records* in a language he could not even read.

Looking back, one can see clearly that changes really began in the late 1980s with Gorbachev's glasnost and perestroika. But glasnost wasn't what we might think of as true openness; it was a policy imposed from the top. I remember smiling to myself as I went from library to library in Russian cities in the late 1980s, looking at exhibits of books from the *spetskhran*, which occurred simultaneously and all looked the same: books by Trotsky and other political leaders who had fallen from favor, novels and poetry by

---

11   Quoted in Marianna Tax Choldin, "Good Business, Bad Business, No Business: Selling Western Books to the Soviets," in *Proceedings of the Second International Conference of Slavic Librarians and Information Specialists*, ed. Choldin (New York: Russica Publishers, 1986).

forbidden authors from the 1920s up to the recent past, and some banned foreign titles. Well, I told myself, better to have all of these identical exhibits than none at all!

The most thrilling moments of my late-late-Soviet experience came in August 1991. Harvey was with me in Moscow, Leningrad, and a number of spots in between while I did my duty as one of four professor-lecturers on a ten-university alumni tour, sailing up the rivers and through the lakes on a delightful East German–built ship, the *SS Krzhizhanovskii*, named after a contemporary of Lenin's known for electrification of the countryside. We sailed right into the attempted coup of August 19–21, 1991. Truly we sailed into history.

On August 19, at about 10:30 in the morning, the ship's first officer sent word that there had been a coup and Gorbachev had been taken. This startling news interrupted the panel discussion my three colleagues and I were presenting to our charges. We were all stunned, needless to say, and one of my colleagues on the panel cracked a joke—"Oh, yes, and Hitler has been sighted in Tel Aviv driving a taxi!"—but the report turned out to be all too true.

That trip, especially those three days, pumped lifeblood and tremendous energy into my research. In my quiet study on the fourth floor of the library, I had read all the books and practiced being a censor. Now, during the first days of the tour, before the coup attempt, we docked in small Russian towns previously closed to foreigners, such as Kizhi, renowned for its stunning array of wooden Orthodox churches. I saw that glasnost had a beachhead on these shores. At a kiosk I bought a movie magazine featuring pictures of naked women, and if that were not enough, on the wall of the kiosk hung an icon of the Madonna partially covered by a *Playboy* calendar.

The day the coup began, I stood on the deck of our tour boat, high on adrenalin, and witnessed Soviet censorship crumbling around me. Down in the ship's lounge, Soviet radio had been silenced; only the solemn sounds of Chopin's funeral march rumbled through the speakers, a common filler during Soviet news blackouts. And Soviet TV showed only the ballet *Swan Lake*, as was the custom whenever a leader died. Nothing else—just *Swan Lake*. On deck we picked up a BBC world broadcast, plus Voice of America and Radio Liberty, the old standard "foreign voices" (as they were called) of the Cold War era. At lunch a young waiter moaned that the good times he had hoped for wouldn't come after all. "Now we'll be like Chile under Pinochet," he intoned, shaking his head sadly. "It's all over."

We landed that afternoon at the ancient island monastery of Valaam, where fearful Orthodox monks in brown cassocks and sandals greeted us, wringing their hands, looking proudly at all the work they had done to restore the ruined buildings and dreading new persecution.

When we arrived in Leningrad, we were taken around the city in a tour bus with speakers blasting rock music and news of the coup, thanks to a Soviet-Norwegian joint-venture radio station, Radio ROKS, that broadcast bits of news between songs. Sometimes during the days of the coup we also heard broadcasts from a new Leningrad station, Radio Otkrytyi Gorod (Open City).

In the square in front of the Leningrad city hall were remnants of a barricade set up during the night to stop the tanks rumored to be on their

Crowd in front of the Leningrad City Soviet during the coup attempt
(August 1991)

way but then dismantled at the passionate request of Mayor Sobchak, who urged peaceful resistance. (The tanks never arrived.) A vast, serious crowd had gathered in front of the building, displaying placards and banners with messages: "Soldiers! Don't spill fraternal blood!" and "Better to die standing than to live on your knees," an old Spanish Civil War slogan. One of my favorites proclaimed: "The new bolshevik putsch will ruin Russia forever! Army! Defend your people against the descendants of hangmen and murderers!" Another favorite bore these words: "We'll survive hardships, but we won't tolerate an illegal regime. Everyone to the defense of the Lensovet. The tanks are 100 km from *Piter*!" (The Lensovet is the city hall; "Piter" is the affectionate diminutive for the beloved city of St. Petersburg.) Some protesters gave me that placard, asking me to take it to America in case the coup failed. The poster now resides in the University of Illinois archives.

While Harvey and I were in Leningrad, Katia was in Moscow, where there were indeed tanks. She and other Soviet librarians happened to be hosting the annual conference of the International Federation of Library Associations and Institutions (IFLA) that week, an enormous and time-consuming job under ordinary circumstances. But Katia also had the coup to tend to. She made the print shop in her library available to people preparing independent newspapers to be posted on walls throughout the city, so the populace might keep up with what was going on despite the news vacuum. At one point a KGB officer entered the premises and asked what was going on. Quaking inside, she informed him calmly that they were printing. He looked around, nodded, advised them to close the shades, and left! And the same day the coup was announced, Katia signed an agreement with the BBC to mount an interactive exhibition in the library, complete with live news feeds. No one challenged her. Great chunks were falling out of that crumbling edifice, the Soviet Union.

The coup was over on the third day. Boris Yeltsin, president of the Russian Republic, stood defiantly on a tank, Gorbachev reappeared, and the mortally wounded Soviet Union lurched into its final decline. Harvey and I, in Leningrad, rejoiced with Liubov' Moiseevna Ravich and her family. Now everyone was calling the city St. Petersburg again and cursing the *bandity* and *razboiniki* (bandits and scoundrels) who had attempted the coup—and then we flew with our tour group to Berlin. When we left the country, my placard from the demonstration came through Soviet customs with no problems, to my surprise and relief. No one was paying attention anymore.

In Berlin we walked, with thousands of others, through the Brandenburg Gate, long a no-man's-land, and viewed the remnants of the wall, which I had last seen intact and complete with guard towers and armed soldiers. I felt dizzy with joy and disbelief. In 1959 Stefan had given me a book about Berlin with the Brandenburg Gate on the cover, and somewhere I had picked up a poster, a view of the gate at night, illumined with the words "*Macht das Tor auf.*" (Open the gate) at the bottom. And now the great gate was open, the miserable wall was rubble, and the Soviet Union was collapsing day by day.

Two months later, I was back in Moscow for a conference convened by the Lenin Library and the Library of Congress. The conference, an activity of the US-Soviet Commission on Library Cooperation (of which I was a member), had originally been scheduled for September 1990, but the first Gulf War broke out and the US government decided we shouldn't travel then. So here I was, in October 1991, enjoying the last rays of the twilight of the Soviet Union.

"Enjoying" is perhaps not the best word to use. Certainly I felt a small amount of schadenfreude as I experienced the collapse. Everything was falling apart. Good! But as soon as I spoke to Galia, I sobered up. One day her mother stood in a queue for seven hours to buy some sugar. There was no milk or clothing for the children; Galia fought back tears as she asked me to bring secondhand clothes for the boys next time I came. (Of course, I brought new clothes, all I could carry.)

Our commission stayed at the famous—infamous, in my view—Hotel Rossiia, adjacent to Red Square. Built in 1967, the Rossiia was supposed to be one of the largest and grandest hotels in the world, with room for four thousand guests. I had stayed there last in July 1987, with the other US members of the US-Soviet Commission on Library Cooperation, and it was a difficult enough place then, earning my personal Hotel to Avoid Gold Medal—but that visit was bliss compared to this one.

October in Moscow can be cold, windy, snowy, and raw, and so it was in 1991. Many of the hotel's windows didn't close properly, so some rooms were little warmer than the outside. Most nights our sleep was interrupted by phone calls from prostitutes seeking business. In the morning we had to chase from one *bufet* to another, traversing what seemed like miles of corridors, to put together a minimal breakfast. We never knew which *bufet* would be open, and indeed the women in charge seemed to enjoy slamming down the metal grate over the counter when they saw us running toward them.

Usually, despite our best efforts, breakfast lacked some key element, such as coffee or bread or cheese. And the *dezhurnye* (women on the floor who keep your room key and supposedly look after you) refused to give us tea or even hot water, although they had enormous samovars in their rooms that were always full of hot water. (This was a shocking change: the *dezhurnye* had always taken care of me before in Soviet hotels, including this one, and I'd brought the obligatory little gifts for them, as I've always done—queen-sized panty hose, chocolates, chewing gum, Marlboros.) So, by the time we were ready to start the day's work, pushing through the crowds of prostitutes and people selling dubious items in the lobby, we were not in the best physical or mental shape. I was always furious, not at all my normal state of mind.

I vowed never to stay at the Rossiia again, but I did, for a couple of nights, in the summer of 2006 and was most pleasantly surprised. A miracle had occurred, and the place worked. It had been privatized, and the owners had closed down most of the building, cutting it to a reasonable size. There were even decent restaurants on the premises. Its new life was brief, though; the hotel proved unmanageable in the end, a great white elephant near Red Square, and was razed. No doubt some people miss it, but I emphatically do not.

The 1991 conference, grandly titled "The National Library in the Life of the Nation," was held in hall number 1 of the House of Unions, a grand, dusty Soviet meeting venue. We were greeted at the opening by Nikolai Gubenko, minister of culture of the USSR, and Robert Strauss, US ambassador to Russia. We worked our way through "Libraries in a Democratic Society," "National Libraries and National Character," "The Historical Legacy and Contemporary Functions," "National Library Support for the National Legislature," and, finally, on the second day—Wednesday, October 30, 1991, at 12:30 p.m.—we arrived at the moment I had been waiting for with great anticipation and an enormous amount of dread: "Access to

Research Materials and Restrictions on Information." My session, where I was to speak to a Soviet audience about Russian and Soviet censorship. I had never done this before.

I was, to put it succinctly, terrified. I had decided to speak from notes rather than read a paper and to take advantage of the simultaneous interpreters and speak English rather than Russian. After this conference I almost always prepared my talks in English and then worked with a translator—either a member of Katia's staff or my colleague in Urbana, the Russian émigré poet Dmitrii Bobyshev—to put them into Russian. But this was my first time. I was fearful of what the consequences might be for me, what punishment I might expect from the Soviet state for talking about a forbidden topic, and I decided to take refuge in my own language, to be relaxed enough to be able to concentrate on communicating with my eyes and body, to read the reactions of my Soviet audience. I don't know what I thought would happen: Would I be shouted at? Would the KGB escort me from the hall? My imagination, honed by years of Soviet horror stories and the censor lurking inside me, went wild.

Nothing happened, of course. I stood up and spoke, clearly and slowly, in short sentences so the interpreters could do their job. Wonder of wonders, my voice didn't shake! I talked about my research on censorship in imperial Russia and laid out my concept of Soviet "omnicensorship." I described my observations of the Gorbachev era and recalled my experiences during the putsch, as Russians often call the attempted coup, only two months earlier. I listed some positive signs: Public discussion about the evils of censorship. Opening of *spetskhrany* all over the country. Formerly party-line media becoming progressive. Privatization of publishing houses. Opening of archives. New schools with new curricula. A military officer, finally able to read Orwell's *1984*, realizing that he had to be against the coup. Solzhenitsyn declaring that he would return to Russia to live, ending years of exile in Vermont.

On the negative side, I mentioned incidents of the independent press being harassed and the related manipulation of the alleged "paper shortage" to discriminate against publications the government didn't like. (The Soviet Union, large parts of which are heavily forested, should have no paper shortage.)

Then I enumerated some signs about which I felt ambivalent: The Russian Writers Union closed because it was too conservative (I'd rather have seen it allowed to function, whatever its politics). The right-wing, nationalist organization Pamiat' (Memory) had a new radio station (this should be permitted, but its message made me very uneasy).

I noted my ambivalence about developments in the religious sphere too. There was a revival of Jewish life. Aaron Lansky, founder of the Jewish Book Center in Amherst, Massachusetts, was bringing Yiddish books to Latvia, Lithuania, and Estonia (still Soviet republics, although they would be independent in a few weeks!). *Taxi Blues*, a 1990 Russian film, addresses anti-Semitism. The Soviet Yiddish-language monthly *Sovetish Heymland* would publish in Russian too, reaching a much wider audience, and in the republic of Moldova (also soon to be independent) a twice-weekly Russian-language paper with a circulation of about ten thousand was aimed at Jews in the region of Bessarabia, a heavily Jewish area. The staff of *Veteran*, a conservative Soviet newspaper aimed at the elderly, voted to make the publication into a progressive weekly, and the old editor, under whom pro-Stalinist and anti-Semitic articles appeared, resigned.

But, I noted, there was an increase in anti-Semitic activities. Various papers had published articles on Hitler and excerpts from *Mein Kampf.* I saw a piece in an independent newspaper thanking Saddam Hussein for bombing Israel and wishing all Jews (an epithet was used) dead.

More ambivalence for me: a Committee for the Protection of Public Morals was formed, with Jewish, Muslim, Buddhist, and Orthodox clergy serving on it. (Why was such a committee needed? Couldn't it be dangerous?) Since August, Lubavitcher Hasidic Jews had been protesting at the Leninka, demanding that twelve thousand books, known as the Shneerson collections (after Rabbi Menachem Mendel Shneerson, head of the Lubavitch movement), confiscated by the state seventy years ago, be returned to the movement. The Soviet Supreme Court ordered the release of the books, but there was no resolution yet. (As a moderate Jew, I'm uneasy with the growing Chasidic presence in Russia, but I do believe strongly in freedom of religion.) I'm also uneasy with the mighty stream of American evangelical Christians into Moscow and other Russian cities. (Many Russians are uneasy too and annoyed; as far as they are concerned, they are already Christians.)

Right after the putsch, Yeltsin closed *Pravda*, the official organ of the Communist Party, and some other papers and centralized the press. I would rather have seen him encourage an independent press. I'm concerned about intellectual freedom in economically and politically unstable times and especially in the absence of the rule of law. I'm not very happy with the continuing distinction between "legal" and "illegal" publications.

I ended my remarks by describing Katia's and my plans for an exhibition on Russian and Soviet censorship and said I hoped to see continuing improvement in the quality of life and progress toward the solution of problems in the area of intellectual freedom. As someone who believes firmly in freedom for all religions, I said I was pleased to see religious institutions starting to function again. It's not necessary, I added, to be Christian in order to feel good about seeing working churches arise out of "museums of atheism" or warehouses, the restoration of desecrated churches, monks living again in monasteries, but I repeated that I'm distressed by the anti-Semitism I'm seeing in Russia. I realize that nothing is simple, but must it be this way?

The audience had listened politely. There were no questions or discussion. My counterpart on the Soviet side, N. P. Igumnova, a deputy director of the Leninka, rose and read her paper. I don't recall exactly what she said, but I believe she spoke about the growing availability of information, thanks to modern technology. (For decades Soviet librarians talked about "availability" and refused to use the term "access," which implies actually giving people material they need.)

After Igumnova's talk and a few uncontroversial remarks by the American and Soviet commentators, the session was over. As we broke for coffee and cookies, I felt like a deflated balloon. What a pathetic failure I am! Here was my first chance to talk about censorship with Soviet citizens, and I couldn't manage to interest even a single person. My usual confidence had evaporated, leaving me feeling sick, discouraged, and jet-lagged.

Until, that is, a man approached me and introduced himself: Vladimir Solodin, chief censor of the Soviet censorship agency, Glavlit! He appreciated my work very much, he said, and wanted me to know that I had gotten it just right. How had I managed to do that, in America? I mumbled something about our wonderful libraries but couldn't say much because my heart was pounding so vigorously.

From that moment on, life improved. At the evening reception two colleagues told me that people were afraid of what I might say in my paper, but I was polite and they weren't upset. One of these colleagues was Inna Baldina, head of the Leninka's *spetskhran*, the country's largest closed repository, with 280,000 foreign volumes. She explained that they had decided to keep the banned publications together, rather than integrating them into the library's collection. The card catalog would remain intact, and readers would have full access to it, as well as to the banned books and magazines. She was agitated because Evgenii Kuzmin, an investigative journalist for the liberal paper *Literaturnaia gazeta*, had taken the Leninka to task for not dissolving the *spetskhran* immediately. He doesn't understand, she told me; it's better this way. Baldina added that she was eager to work with Katia and me on the censorship exhibition. My head was spinning.

The next day I had lunch with Katia and one of her staff members, Viktor Moskvin. This was an amazing lunch. I pinched myself under the table. Viktor and I were to curate the censorship exhibition. Like me, he had written on imperial Russian censorship of foreign books. Surely, he hasn't published anything, I thought to myself. This is still the Soviet Union! Viktor proposed October 27, 2002, at 4 p.m., for the Moscow opening. He wanted to commission a documentary film to accompany the Soviet part of the exhibition, with funding from the Soros Foundation and other sources. We would get material from all the important Soviet libraries. At the opening we would have interviews, lectures, and roundtables on censorship in Russia and the Soviet Union. Maurice Friedberg would come, as well as other foreign specialists. We would publish the proceedings; I would write the preface. We would take the exhibition on tour, to St. Petersburg, of course (no one calls it Leningrad anymore), and to Kiev, Irkutsk, the Baltics. By the end of lunch I felt faint.

I spent the afternoon at Katia's library with her and two of her deputies, Evgeniia Rosinskaia (Zhenia) and Galina Kislovskaia (Galia), both of whom became dear friends. The Library for Foreign Literature was nothing like my memory from 1987, when I visited briefly with the Commission on Library Cooperation. Now Katia and her progressive crew were in charge and the institution was no longer Soviet, although the country would still exist for two more months. They took me on a tour of the building, which was being remodeled by a British contractor, David Whitwell. I saw the BBC exhibition, with its telephones through which you could hear the Queen's English and its live BBC broadcast.

Late in the tour we stepped into a small, cheerful, sunlit room designated as the new Children's Reading Room. What was it before? I asked. Katia smiled beatifically, with just a touch of impishness. "The *spetskhran*," she said.

Former *spetskhran* at the Library for Foreign Literature, transformed into a reading room for children

Before parting, Katia and I set a date for my next visit, in February, when we would begin to work on the exhibition in earnest. She urged me to stay with her, as we would be working closely together. I demurred politely; she insisted. You know our hotels, she said. Why live miserably when you could be with us? I accepted, of course. We both sensed our new bond: we had moved beyond collegiality to something very strong and warm, utterly compelling. We had entered each other's stories. My Soviet censor was still there, but he took a backseat to Katia.

CHAPTER 7

MY SOVIET PLANET

In 1960, when I made my first trip to the Soviet Union, I had been a Russian-studies baby. Everything excited me during that summer and my college years. Then came Bangladesh and babies, East Lansing, and Champaign-Urbana. By the mid-1970s I had been transformed into a Slavic librarian with a lot of book learning and research experience under my belt. I read and comprehended Russian really well, but I didn't speak it very much; most of the native speakers around me were émigrés trying to improve their English. My two planets orbited steadily and separately, as they had for decades.

In the Soviet Union, the Khrushchev era, which I like to think of as the Decade of Euphoria, in memory of Maurice, had come and gone, and the stagnation era was a solid, stolid presence. I felt stagnant too, resigned to living on my planet and studying the other one from afar, along with many of my Western colleagues. Those who spent a semester or two doing dissertations or advanced research in Moscow or Leningrad, mostly in history and literature, came back with tales of their triumphs and miseries in the archives; their struggles in the dorms, including broken marriages (life was tough for couples in Soviet dorm rooms); the adventures of their daily existence. When they came home, some got jobs as professors at universities around the country. Others were gobbled up by our intelligence services; this was, after all, the Cold War. Wearing my librarian hat and working with the world community of Slavic librarians, I was delighted to help my colleagues locate the materials they needed for their research.

It was a good life. In 1972 we spent the summer in London. Our charter flight had been canceled shortly before we were to depart, and our travel agent managed to book us on the *SS France* instead, not a bad switch at all. The twins, now seven, acquired a lifelong taste for Brie and Camembert in the children's dining room, while Harvey and I feasted on heavenly French cuisine with the grown-ups. Once in London, Harvey spent his days in the India Office archives, following up on some Bangladesh research, and I froze in the British Museum Reading Room, doing research on Russian bibliographers of the nineteenth and early twentieth centuries and writing short articles about them for an encyclopedia. I hadn't expected such cold in the middle of summer and on workdays wrapped myself in every bit of warm clothing I'd brought with me. I also took frequent tea breaks in the museum café and strolled through the galleries of Egyptian, Greek, and Roman art to jump-start my circulation.

Kate and Mary toured the city, sometimes with us and often with a kindly grandmother from New Zealand visiting her English family who lived across the street from us in Highgate. At the end of the summer we traveled to Germany—my first visit since 1960—so Harvey and the girls could meet my old friends and their young families in Bielefeld and Esslingen. We flew out of Frankfurt on the day after the attack on the Israeli athletes at the Munich Olympics, a somber ending to a delightful summer.

It was a bittersweet return to Germany for me. In the twelve years I'd been away, the *Wirtschaftswunder*, or economic miracle, had occurred; the physical recovery from the war was remarkable, and people lived well. And German society was changing. *Gastarbeiter*, guest workers from Yugoslavia and Turkey, were everywhere, doing the jobs affluent Germans no longer wanted or needed to do. New little restaurants serving spicy food had sprung up; people with dark hair and eyes mingled with blonde, blue-eyed Germans; and exotic languages were heard on the streets.

Back in Champaign, my Illinois colleagues and I started the Summer Research Lab in 1973, attracting Slavic scholars from all over the world to campus to use our rich collections and consult with our librarians. In 1976 we launched the Slavic Reference Service and began helping scholars at their own institutions find what they needed for their research, wherever in the world it might be. And two years later, eighteen years after my first trip, I returned to the Soviet Union.

My seven trips between 1978 and 1991 opened my eyes, heightened my pulse, and sent my emotions flying high and sinking low, sometimes simultaneously. I recall many things about those trips, memory aided by the Sol Tax–inspired notes I took during each trip. Recurring themes: Jewishness; sovietization; deprivation; and, of course, my growing awareness of omni-censorship through real-life experiences.

Harvey and I were both scheduled to be in Europe for a couple of weeks in August 1978; I was meeting with Slavic librarians, and he would attend a sociology conference in Sweden. We met in Stockholm and flew to Helsinki together, where I had arranged to visit the famous Helsinki University Library Russian collection, developed between 1809 and 1917, when Finland was part of the Russian Empire. Luckily for Russian scholars in the West, during those years the Helsinki University Library was an official depository, which meant that a copy of every book published within the empire had to be deposited there. So when the Soviets closed the borders, Finland and its great collection remained in the West, on our planet, providing open access to its treasures. Our library in Urbana was involved in a huge project with the publisher University Microfilms to copy and make available the Helsinki volumes most needed by scholars. I loved the fact that, thanks to the twists and turns of history, this library had ended up on our planet. The Soviets might be able to control what we saw inside their country, but they couldn't keep us out of the Helsinki University Library. One up for access, one down for censorship!

Traveling to Leningrad on that August day in 1978 was an unforgettable adventure. We traveled by train from Helsinki, and at the Finnish-Soviet border some military types—customs officers? border police? soldiers?—boarded the train and searched thoroughly in overhead compartments and under the seats. What or whom they were looking for, I don't know. They did, however, ask explicitly, in English, whether we had "books or magazines for Soviet people." They didn't challenge us, but after they left our compartment, my fear of crossing Soviet borders, which had begun in Moscow in 1960 because of that little icon Vladimir had given me, was now thoroughly ensconced in my psyche.

Harvey was also unnerved, and I believe this was the first chink in his armor. A sociologist with strong liberal leanings, he had always listened with gently raised eyebrows when I talked about the Soviet Union, certain it wasn't as bad as I claimed. But when he disembarked from that train in the

Finland Station and looked around him, the episode in our compartment fresh in his mind, he saw with his own eyes the glum terrain of the other planet, with its shabby station and unsmiling people wearing ill-fitting clothes. There at the station, a few minutes into his first visit to the Soviet Union, he asked me a plaintive question that was to become famous in our family: "Couldn't you have gone into Italian studies?"

We were in Leningrad for only three days, but it seemed like a lifetime. We visited the old Imperial Public Library, in Soviet times named after the Russian writer Saltykov-Shchedrin (who had nothing whatever to do with the library) and known as the Saltykovka. Today it's the Russian National Library, fondly known as the Publichka. Several of my Russian bibliographers, subjects of my encyclopedia articles, had worked here, and I was fascinated by its grand imperial structure. Founded by Catherine the Great, the library was loaded with rare books and manuscripts, including Voltaire's library, priceless volumes expropriated from Poland, and numerous other treasures. A tiny woman of a certain age who had spent years in the United States with her family before the war and spoke excellent English with a New York accent showed us around. I met the Acquisitions Department people who worked with our library and arranged to pick up a microfilm ordered by one of our graduate students. I was proud to have conducted my first professional business in Russia successfully, although I wasn't proud of my spoken Russian, which was tentative and filled with long, awkward pauses while I groped for words.

On the second day of our stay I had the first of what were to be many memorable visits with Ravich. I had formed a relationship with her by correspondence a few years earlier, while I was writing a series of short encyclopedia articles on prominent prerevolutionary Russian bibliographers. One of them, Grigorii Gennadi, interested me particularly, and in my search for Russian-language sources on him I came across Ravich's name. I learned that she was a professor at the Institute of Culture in Leningrad, where librarianship was taught, along with a number of other subjects in the area of "cultural management." On an impulse I had written to her, and to my delight I received a very nice answer.

Ravich was a small, stout Jewish woman who lived with her daughter, Marianna, and her granddaughter, Katia, in a *kommunal'naia*, a communal apartment in the Dostoevsky District of Leningrad. Hers was the only *kommunal'naia* I ever visited during my many trips to Russia, and it made a deep impression on Harvey and me. The family had one room in a fifth-floor walk-up that had, in prerevolutionary times, been a single-family apartment. They shared the kitchen and bathroom with other families and stuffed all their belongings into that one small room. The *kommunal'naia* was a Soviet institution that lingers on in the present, due to an ongoing housing shortage in Russian cities.

Ravich complained bitterly about her living conditions. Walking up all those flights of stairs strained her bad heart; the neighbors were mean, anti-Semitic, and *nekul'turnyi*, uncultured, a terrible insult from an educated Russian. She had applied to the authorities repeatedly, citing her heart condition and, more important, her status as a "hero of the Great Patriotic War," the Soviet term for World War II, which hit the Soviet Union incredibly hard. (Leningrad was one of the hardest-hit cities, enduring starvation during the infamous Blockade.) She had a handful of medals of which she was very proud; she showed them to me every time I came.

Years later, in August 1991, Harvey and I were finally able to visit her family in their new single-family apartment. It seemed the lap of luxury. Everyone was in a euphoric state that day, the final hours of the attempted coup that would have toppled Gorbachev. How pleasant to share the euphoria with an old friend whose life had taken a turn for the better!

I saw Ravich numerous times after our first meeting, whenever my work took me to Leningrad (or St. Petersburg, as it became once again after the Soviet Union collapsed). Her energy and enthusiasm for her work never flagged; I received new articles and books of hers regularly. She had a sixtieth birthday "jubilee," as is the Russian custom, and her students and colleagues made a fuss over her when she retired. She continued to do research and publish even as her health declined.

During our first time together, in 1978, we had gone for a walk through one of Leningrad's famous gardens. It was too dangerous to talk inside, she had told me; in her apartment, if I strayed too close to certain topics. . . . She pointed significantly at the ceiling and shook her head. While we were walking in the garden, I shared with her my plans for a dissertation on imperial Russian censorship. I'll always remember how she stopped, fixed me with an incredulous stare, and told me I was crazy to pick that topic. Why not stay with something safe, like nineteenth-century bibliography? She shook her head sadly and told me that she wouldn't be able to help me get material from the archives: it was simply an impossible topic. When I insisted that this was what I wanted to do, she sighed, patted my arm, and said she understood. And she did try to help me get something from an archive but to no avail.

Over the years I always brought her copies of my articles on censorship, which she accepted eagerly. She couldn't read English but found someone to translate for her. When *A Fence around the Empire* was published in Russian in 2002,[1] I made sure she received a copy, and in December 2003 I received the most beautiful letter from her, including these words about the book, which I treasure:

> This is a magnificent thing; there has never been anything even remotely like it in Russian book studies. Everything is there: depth of research and feeling for the times (in my opinion, a priceless quality), and simply so very many most interesting facts. I knew some of this before, but much was new and even unexpected.

I visited for the last time not long before her death. Ravich had lost the edge of her sharpness, but it was still possible to have an engrossing conversation with her. She always wanted to know about Harvey and our daughters and, of course, my research.

In her final years Ravich worried about having enough money to pay for her funeral. Life had been hard for her all the years I knew her; she was retired from her institute, and pensions were pitifully small. Her daughter, Marianna, earned practically nothing as a librarian at the Academy of Sciences Library. Each time I visited, I left money with Marianna, first to help with the costs of daily life and later for the funeral. When Katia called in 2006 and told me that Ravich had died, I wept for my Leningrad Jewish auntie, my mentor and supporter, a brave and admirable woman.

---

1   The Russian edition of *A Fence around the Empire* (Zabor vokrug imperii) was published in Moscow by Rudomino Publishers in 2002.

Looking back on those August days in 1978, I realize with some surprise that our encounters with Soviet Jews are what I remember most vividly. I hadn't expected that meeting Ravich and the families of our young émigré friends in Urbana, all Jews, would have had such an emotional kick. Ravich looked at Harvey and said—in Russian, since she knew no English—"What a lovely Jewish face he has!" One of the émigré's moms asked when our families had left Russia for the United States, and when we explained that our grandparents had emigrated around 1900, she smiled ruefully and remarked that they were the smart ones.

On each of my subsequent visits to the Soviet Union and post-Soviet Russia after 1978, my Jewish antennae were up and quivering. Many of my new friends were Jewish, or half Jewish, or formerly Jewish. Many of the dishes I ate at their kitchen tables could have been served in my house. They loved bagels. They sprinkled their conversations with Yiddish words and phrases, the same ones used at home. They even looked like members of my family. But some of these friends were fearful in ways I never had to be. I'll never forget a conversation during a Soviet-American meeting in Moscow in the early 1980s. We went around the table and introduced ourselves. When my turn came, I mentioned in passing that "Choldin" is a name that was invented by immigration officers when my husband's father entered the United States in 1912. Like many Jewish immigrants of that period, his family's name, difficult for the immigration officer to pronounce, was simply changed: "Kholodenko" became "Choldin." During our coffee break, a young woman took me aside, looked earnestly and quite intensely into my eyes, and advised me not to repeat this story in the Soviet Union. "It's not good to draw attention to your Jewishness," she said gently, in Russian, and in her eyes I read depths of pain and humiliation.

Something else that fascinated and frustrated me in the 1980s is what I think of as the "sovietization" of our country during the Cold War. Now that the Soviet Union has been gone for more than twenty years, much of the feel, the smell, the texture, the jargon, and the *anekdoty* of the Cold War period has faded or been wiped out altogether. People who came of age after the collapse may not know that throughout the Soviet period, the only way Western scholars could make research trips to the Soviet Union and the countries of Eastern and Central Europe under Soviet "protection" was to do so under the umbrella of an "official" organization, governmental or with close ties to government. In the United States, that organization was IREX, the International Research and Exchanges Board, founded in 1968 on the basis of a program that had been established soon after Stalin's death by a group of US universities to administer exchange programs. All Western countries had their own equivalents of IREX so their scholars could spend time in Soviet-bloc countries for research purposes, and so scholars from countries on the other planet could have a channel for their own research visits to Western countries.

The US and Soviet governments cooperated on scholarly exchanges so each side could get what it wanted. The Soviets sent scientists in engineering and the physical and natural sciences to US universities, to update their knowledge and skills in our classrooms and labs. Under Stalin they had lost ground and were unable to take part in the world scientific community, a near-fatal blow to Soviet science. And within Russia, some fields had been nearly destroyed during those years by the influence of insane policies and interpretations on the Russian scientific community. Mendelian genetics, for example, had been forbidden; only the theories of agronomist and biologist Trofim Lysenko, one of Stalin's favorites, were permitted. Because Lysenko rejected Mendel, all scientists had to reject modern genetics as well.

Few, if any, Soviet social scientists or humanists were permitted to visit our planet. Scholars in these fields were seen as politically unreliable, and several of their fields had been abolished or reconfigured into a Marxist-Leninist mold. Western sociology and psychology, hot fields in the West, were at best dormant in the Soviet Union. Later, as glasnost emerged, IREX served also as the US counterpart to various Soviet governmental bodies, enabling us to work together on projects. In this sense, we Americans "sovietized" ourselves, creating a quasi-governmental structure to work within, and it functioned very well for many years. We may not have liked it—I certainly didn't—but we had no choice if we wanted to get anything done. Diplomats have probably always had to endure official meetings where seating is at a long table, Americans on one side, Soviets on the other, with small US and Soviet flags marking our respective territories. Librarians shouldn't have to.

When considering life on the Soviet planet, I could write a lengthy article, maybe even a whole book, about "Deprivation in the Era of Stagnation." I'd include a section on Borders and Travel, one on Food and Goods, and probably some other sections too, but let's look at these, beginning with borders.

Soviet borders are a particular nightmare of mine. I don't know why they affect me so strongly; maybe it's because international travel has always been so easy for me and for my family, friends, and colleagues. But I think it's more than just ease. I've always taken for granted that it's my right to cross the US border and be in other countries and, furthermore, that doing so is a good thing. Papa traveled widely and frequently for what I considered to be excellent reasons: to establish an international community of colleagues. I did the same, on a smaller scale, in the 1980s. Moreover, my sister, Susan, and her husband, Les, went frequently to Spain and lived and worked there as anthropologists, sometimes for as long as a year at a time. Most of the people I knew while growing up traveled beyond our borders, for work and for pleasure, to see the world, to experience other cultures, and to meet people different from themselves. I couldn't imagine living in a place that forbade its citizens to travel beyond its borders. In the course of more than fifty Soviet and post-Soviet border crossings, I never had trouble, not even once. But I worried about it every single time and continue to do so.

In the Food and Goods section of my imagined book on Soviet Deprivation and Stagnation, I'd like to consider cheese. It's October 1991. I've just come back from Moscow, and I'm standing in the cheese department of a shiny new supermarket in Champaign, weeping and remembering. On the other planet, Moscow appears to be going under. Glasnost and perestroika, those reforms from the top, produce wondrous, heady sensations in my friends—librarians, journalists, and other intellectuals—but Soviet life as they knew it is grinding to a halt, and they are suffering. It's been a cold, wet October in Moscow, and as I stand at the cheese counter in Champaign, I recall how the windows in my crumbling hotel room, rimmed with frost, didn't shut. There was no food for breakfast, and prostitutes roamed the lobby and halls. Worse, my friend Galia couldn't find milk for her baby in any store, no matter how enterprising she, her mother, and her mother-in-law were about finding lines to stand in.

Now here I stand, jet-lagged and miserable from a cold. My head and my heart are still with my friends in Moscow. And in front of me is this incredible cheese department, with dozens—maybe hundreds—of brands and types and sizes and shapes, sliced and unsliced, flavored and plain, hard and soft, gathered from all over the world. Furthermore, beyond the cheese department are fresh fruits and vegetables—I need hardly tell you about the variety there—and beyond that meats of every kind, as well as breads and cereals. I'm overcome with sadness and guilt. In the late 1980s I once stood in a government food store (the only kind there was) and stared at a block of yellow cheese, all by itself in the glass case. "What kind of cheese is that?" I asked the unsmiling employee behind the counter. "Soviet cheese," she said, grimly.

On that same visit, I asked an employee in one of Moscow's largest branches of Dom Knigi, the state bookstore, whether there were any works by Chekhov or Tolstoy. (I knew there weren't because I'd looked, but I wanted to hear her answer.) She stared at me in disbelief and replied angrily, "Of course not! Not one single item." I used to buy Soviet editions of Russian classics in the States from Victor Kamkin, the "official" dealer in Washington, DC, and then mail them to Ravich in Leningrad. I even had Kamkin send her some books while I was in Bangladesh. How absurd! How devastating! Why did I have so much and they so little?

Among Goods, let's also consider birth control and children's toys. When I traveled to Russia in the 1980s, I always filled my suitcase with practical gifts for friends: vitamins, aspirin, jeans, powdered milk—and lots of condoms. Abortion was the favored means of birth control in the Soviet Union—at least for ordinary people there were no condoms, no pill, no IUDs, and nothing but abortion—and I did my part to help women friends avoid that particular trauma. Also in my suitcase were clothes for Galia's younger son's favorite toy, a Barbie doll. (I brought a Ken doll too, complete with clothes, which he accepted happily.) I'm so grateful that Soviet customs officers left me alone, as I had no idea how I would have explained those suitcases full of condoms and Barbie outfits. (Probably I would have spoken only English and told the truth, hoping to come off as a silly woman who meant no harm.) Galia and I laugh about it today, but believe me, it was no laughing matter then!

There were some consumer goods available in the Soviet Union, especially in Moscow and Leningrad and a handful of cities foreigners were allowed to visit, but ordinary Soviet citizens were permitted to enter these special shops, called *beriozki* (little birch trees) only when accompanying foreigners, and they weren't allowed to purchase anything there for themselves. Soviets couldn't enter hotels for foreigners either, unless they happened to be highly placed or prostitutes. The system, copied throughout the Soviet world, was demeaning, and I hated it.

I'll conclude this chapter with Galia Levina's story, a Soviet story.

I've had several long, intimate talks with her since we met more than thirty years ago, and I've learned a great deal from her about the texture of life in the Soviet Union. I've read many accounts of other people's lives, memoirs filled with similar details, but Galia is my friend. When she looks at me and tells me about herself and her family and friends, it penetrates as a stranger's story, read in a book, cannot. Galia's is an ordinary story about an educated family. Tolstoy begins *Anna Karenina* with the observation that happy families are all alike, but each unhappy family is unhappy in its own way. This is true of Soviet families as well.

Galia Levina

Like so many of her generation, Galia experienced Stalin's terror as a little girl through friends and family. She came of age in the eras of Euphoria and Stagnation and now lives, with many ups and downs, in post-Soviet Russia. Her Soviet story, in which she describes her family and milieu and the appalling experiences of her friend and teacher, Raia, brings those decades to life for those of us who lived on the other planet.

Galia was an English-language translator on the staff of INION, the Soviet Academy of Sciences institute that dealt with information and documentation in the social sciences (which, in the Marxist scheme of things, included the humanities as well). INION was partner to a group of US librarians and information specialists, including me, who came to the Soviet Union under the auspices of IREX in 1983; we and our Soviet counterparts formed a "binational commission," one of the products of sovietization. Galia and another young woman were assigned to be with our group every waking moment for the two weeks of our visit. (Most of my American colleagues knew no Russian.) In the ordinary course of things, she and her colleagues, all young women with university degrees in English, spent their days writing abstracts, in Russian, of the thousands of English-language social science and humanities journal articles arriving at INION, mainly from exchange-partner libraries in the United States and the United Kingdom.

Galia appealed to me from the moment we met. She had a pleasant round face, intelligent eyes, and a ready smile; her energy and enthusiasm were infectious. Her English, quite British, was fluent—much better than my Russian then and now—and she was always ready to help in either language.

Once during that visit to Moscow I put Galia's new friendship with me to the ultimate test. Papa had become friendly with Ol'ga Sergeevna Akhmanova, a well-known linguist and English-language specialist, one of his advisors during his *Current Anthropology* stays in Moscow, and urged me to meet her. Galia had been Akhmanova's student at Moscow State University, and she was absolutely terrified by her eminent professor. But she was assigned to accompany me, so she did.

Galia reminds me that we had made a plan before the visit: I would do all the talking, in English, and she would remain silent, speaking only

Russian if she had to talk at all. I found the visit quite pleasant, apart from Galia's obvious terror. We came to Akhmanova's apartment, in an old building in central Moscow, for tea one evening. Like many Moscow and Leningrad apartments belonging to intellectuals that I was to visit in the course of my travels, Akhmanova's was filled with heavy Victorian-style furniture—armchairs, armoires, china cupboards, velvet-covered sofas, lace doilies everywhere, and old oriental rugs on the floors. On the walls and tables were family photographs, and bookshelves took up whatever wall space remained.

We had our tea, from a traditional samovar, and sipped vodka; I drank sparingly, as I don't drink, but one didn't refuse Akhmanova. She served us black caviar too, the finest sort, which I, alas, did not appreciate; I've never liked caviar and managed to choke down only a tiny swallow. When she fixed eagle eyes on Galia and interrogated her about her work at INION, I was glad I wasn't her victim! But I was safe, the American daughter of her esteemed colleague. To this day I treasure the Russian-English dictionary, for which she was the chief compiler, that bears the name of Akhmanova's famous husband, Professor Smirnitskii, and that she had sent home for me with Papa inscribed, in her bold hand, "To Marianna Tax, with best wishes from Ol'ga Akhmanova, Moscow, 29 September 1962." To this day Galia turns pale when I remind her of our visit to Akhmanova.

In a brief detour from Galia's story, I'm including a note Papa wrote about Akhmanova after visiting her in June 1963, twenty years before Galia's and my visit, during a *Current Anthropology* trip Papa made to Leningrad and Moscow. He and Akhmanova were contemporaries, and it's interesting to learn his impressions of her and her surroundings. I recently reread the long letter Papa sent home from London (the same letter in which he described my poor friend Vladimir's problems with his party bosses). As was Papa's usual practice, he wrote a combined family letter and field notes, filling both sides of sheets of hotel stationery (this time the once-elegant Metropol, opposite the Bolshoi Theater)—twenty-two pages of small writing and no margins—with a carbon copy for himself.[2]

---

2   Letter from Sol Tax to Gertrude Tax in Chicago, June 22, 1963. University of Chicago Library Archives, Sol Tax Papers, Box 11.

Papa spent the better part of two days with Akhmanova, in her Moscow apartment and in her dacha outside the city. As I recall my visit to Akhmanova with Galia, I enjoyed reading Papa's description of her and her apartment. He had to get there by Metro, alone and knowing no Russian, because all the streets around the hotel were closed for a parade honoring the cosmonauts. (He was an intrepid traveler, and Akhmanova had given him good directions; he writes that he found the place without difficulty.) He wrote:

Olga Akhmanova I expected to be a great character, and I was not disappointed. . . . She is a genuine leader in her profession; she is head of the English Dept. of the University [Moscow State University/mtc]—her dictionary has sold over 10,000,000 copies in the Soviet Union—and she is involved in many causes in the intellectual world. She is the first contact I have had with somebody who appears to feel completely secure, and she says so. She is a great idealist; and she proudly lives in a "communal house." What does this mean? Before the Revolution the well-to-do people had large 6, 8, or 10 room apartments in apartment buildings (as we had and have), but the many poor people "lived in basements." After the Revolution, the many moved into the apartments, and the pattern was sharing bath and kitchen and each family having a room. We read much about that. Since the War there have been built these large apartment houses, in which people have full and private quarters. Virtually all the well-to-do people have by now moved into apartments but Olga stays put. Her husband died eight years ago; they had two sons; I presume the whole family lived in the room. The room is large, and divided into 2 parts. What I presume are beds become in the daytime large and attractive divans in the front (window) part of the room. The other part has a table around which at least half a dozen can dine. The whole is rich with pictures, hangings, interesting furnishings; it is very homey, and one hardly feels sorry for her. Yet there are six families sharing the bathroom and the kitchen, and though she may be used to this, it must still be a nuisance. Anyway, she is proud of her idealism. . . . She was born in 1908, and learned English in school; not until 1956 did she go to England (Oxford) for a few days or weeks. During the 20 years of Isolation, she became recognized as the expert on English, and thus was important to the nation. As she says, this forced her to work hard really to become expert. She is intensely loyal to Communism, as an ideology; critical (as all are) of the faults of the bureaucracy, angry at the "personality cult" era that unjustly and unnecessarily isolated the people from foreigners. A few years ago I could not have been invited to her house, she said; any contact with foreigners was impossible during the "personality cult"; I suppose it is her strong personal reaction and desire for contacts that make her so enthusiastic about CA.

When Galia and I visited Akhmanova in 1983, she was no longer living in a communal apartment; she had the entire unit. Did she move into another building, or at some point did the other families relocate? I don't know the answer. Incidentally, I once heard a rumor that Akhmanova was anti-Semitic; if so, she never revealed it to Galia, me, or Papa, who was a sensitive and astute interviewer.

During subsequent visits to Moscow in the last years of the Soviet Union, I came to know Galia's husband and her two boys quite well. Iura, her husband, worked for a governmental architectural institute making models. He was very artistic and decorated the walls of their apartment with a wonderful, colorful mural. When the Soviet Union collapsed, the institute collapsed too, like many others, and Iura never found another suitable job. He worked for some years as a porter at the Hotel Ukraina, one of Moscow's seven Stalinist "wedding cake" skyscrapers. This is the same Ukraina where my family had stayed in August 1960, with those temperamental elevators. Like many Soviet hotels, the Ukraina fell upon hard times and was in a state of perpetual *remont* (repair); according to Galia, its current owners had stripped the vast building of its original high-quality furnishings and fixtures and replaced them with junk.

Over the years I watched Galia's sons grow up, study, and survive military service (a real horror for Galia, who feared her younger son would be sent to Chechnya and so pulled whatever strings she could to keep him in the Moscow area). At her dacha (weekend home outside the city), where she maintains a large garden planted years ago by her late mother, Galia relaxed and recovered from the stress of Moscow life. Each year Harvey bought flower and vegetable seeds for the garden and I would carry the packets to

Galia, who planted them and reported on their progress. (We used to call this "the International Tomato Project," as we started with tomatoes, but soon we expanded to all manner of flora that would, we hoped, thrive in the short northern growing season.) In the new Russia, Galia has access to all kinds of seeds, but we still bring her some, for old times' sake. . . .

The dacha came to Galia's family through her mother's father, an eminent crystallographer and member of the Academy of Sciences. In her grandfather's time, academicians were rewarded with dachas in elite communities outside Moscow, Leningrad, and other Soviet cities. His is in Abramtsevo, a well-known community with roots in pre-Soviet times where his neighbors were also scientists, scholars, artists, and writers.

Galia talked often and affectionately about this grandfather, Nikolai Vasil'evich Belov, to whom she was very close. In October 1991, she asked me whether I would send greetings to an old friend and colleague of his in the United States, along with a medal issued recently by the Soviet Academy of Sciences to honor her grandfather posthumously in his centenary year. (He died in 1982, just before I met Galia; how sad I am that I wasn't able to meet him!) Of course, I agreed to be a courier, as I always did, and was startled, going through my papers on the plane home, to see that Galia had given me the name and home address of one of our most famous scientists, Nobel Laureate Linus Pauling! I sent Pauling, then ninety years old, the medal, and not long after that I received a letter from him recalling their friendship. (The medal is now in the Museum of Natural History at the University of Illinois in Urbana.)

Her grandfather, Galia told me, had been a very religious man who attended church all his life, despite the dangers of doing so in Soviet times. (Scholars were afraid to even mention the word "church," she noted, much less go to one.) He never joined the Communist Party either, and Galia says it's a miracle that he was allowed to continue his studies as a young man and even to go abroad starting in 1954, after Stalin's death. In the 1930s, the dangerous years, someone anonymously denounced him to the secret police, and had he not left Leningrad for Moscow, he might have shared the fate of many other scientists at that time. After that he spent his distinguished career at the Institute of Crystallography in Moscow, where he also survived more denunciations, perhaps because he was acknowledged worldwide as an expert in his field and his work was important for the national interest. Or perhaps it was simply good luck; one never knew in those days.

Belov's life under Stalin had been difficult; he earned a small salary and constantly feared for his own life and his family's, and he was the envy of his colleagues, which is what led to the denunciations. Moreover, he wrote "for the drawer," unable to publish many of his works. The family had very little money but managed to survive. He may have been protected by the director of his institute, who didn't want to lose one of his best scientists.

Galia said it was difficult for her to say much about that time because her grandfather and parents almost never spoke about Stalin when she was a little girl: "They were afraid. They were afraid to speak in my presence. I instinctively felt their hatred for and fear of that monster and his gang and their disappointment with the whole system, but when my grandpa started saying something 'wrong,' my grandmother immediately switched to French. The fear during the Stalin era became so great that even many years later every piece of paper, every envelope, every letter from that time that my grandparents wanted to throw away had to be torn into small pieces."

Too young to have experienced the worst times, Galia still carries her family's history with her, and as time passed, she absorbed the terrible stories of friends as well. Earlier in her life, before her challenging studies with the hard-driving Ol'ga Akhmanova, Galia had another English teacher, Raissa Aleksandrovna Rubenstein (nickname Raia), whose story she told me only recently, as I was beginning work on this memoir. I didn't know Raia personally, but I've read and heard stories like hers too many times. It's so easy to grow numb from these stories, to walk away saying, "Oh, yes, here's another victim of Stalinism." One can lose the individual faces as they blend into a mass portrait of victims. But Galia has taken Raia, her teacher and friend, into herself. She loved and respected her, and when, in the late 1980s, she learned Raia's terrible story, she absorbed it and would never forget it. She honored Raia's memory when she told me about her, knowing that I would write a little about Raia and, in so doing, I would help provide a little piece of the immortality to which Raia is surely entitled.

Raia's parents, Jews, had emigrated to the United States when she was three years old, at the beginning of the twentieth century, when my own grandparents emigrated. Galia estimates that she was born in 1900 or 1902. Raia and her siblings grew up on our planet, bilingual in Russian and English, but always dreamed of returning to Russia. They fulfilled their dream in 1934. Raia found a job immediately, teaching English to Communist Party leaders and bureaucrats—her Russian was better than theirs—at the Institut krasnoi professury (Institute of Red Professors) in Moscow. She lived a good and happy life until one hot summer day in 1937 or 1938, when her world collapsed. This was the beginning of Stalin's "Great Purges"; Raia would have been in her late thirties.

Her students were writing an exam when armed soldiers burst into the room and arrested Raia. She was brought to Butyrka Prison, from prerevolutionary times an infamous transit prison for political prisoners and others waiting to be sent into exile in Siberia or, in Soviet times, to the gulag. Butyrka was known for its brutal regime; in this period, waves of twenty thousand prisoners at a time were incarcerated here, and thousands were shot after their "trials." Raia was interrogated throughout the day and night, standing the entire time, with only some water to drink. (Her legs never recovered.) In the morning she found the strength to ask the interrogator why she had been arrested. "You are accused of being a British spy," he responded. "But I've never been to Great Britain," she protested. "Then where were you all those years?" "In the USA," she said. "Oh," he said, with evident relief: "It doesn't matter—a spy is a spy"! Raia's legs collapsed, and she fainted, regaining consciousness only when the interrogator poured cold water on her.

Raia was kept in the prison hospital until she was sent to Siberia on a filthy and crowded ship. She ended up in a camp near the Siberian city of Tomsk, where she remained until the late 1940s, when she was released and allowed to live in Tomsk and even to teach. After Stalin's death in March 1953, she was finally allowed to return to Moscow. She was allotted a room in a communal apartment, on the fifth floor, with no elevator, just like my friend Ravich in Leningrad. Because of her poor health and ruined legs, it was extremely difficult for her to live there, so sometime in the early 1960s she moved in with her friend Natal'ia Albertovna Volzhina, a well-known translator of the fiction of Dickens, Poe, Scott, Faulkner, and other American and British authors.

Not being practical women, Raia and Natal'ia didn't plan for the future, and as it happened, Natal'ia died first, in the early 1970s. Raia continued to live in the apartment, but illegally, without the papers giving her the right to stay there. One day in 1979 or 1980, when Raia was in her early eighties and in very poor health, officials came to the apartment and told her she must leave immediately. She tried to explain that she needed time to transfer all the books—hundreds, perhaps thousands, of them—to her old room in the communal apartment, but the officials were indifferent. "One week or we'll throw everything in the street!"

Reluctantly, because she had never asked Galia for a favor before, Raia appealed to her for help. Galia turned immediately to her grandfather, who mobilized his academician friends and appealed on Raia's behalf to Roald Sagdeev, an internationally known scientist and a very influential man, a deputy of the Supreme Soviet, the top Soviet legislative body. Thanks to these powerful connections, Raia was allowed to stay in Natal'ia's apartment until her death in 1983.

Galia wrote me this final story about Raia, and I could feel her rage and sadness as she typed the e-mail message. Raia's brother married an English girl and went to Britain before 1937, and her sister managed to leave for the United States before Raia's arrest. Raia went to visit her sister in the mid-1970s. She was surprised that the authorities gave her an American visa so easily. (At that time getting an American visa with such a "past"—prisoner, relatives abroad, and Jewish—was a miracle!) Candidly, they explained that they didn't care about giving a visa to a person her age, nor did they care whether such an old lady ever came back. What kind of state, Galia asked, treats its citizens this way? And I say to myself: how inexpressibly painful that my friends had to live under this oppressive shadow, black clouds hovering over them, obliterating the sun. By virtue of our friendship they have drawn me in too, and we huddle together in the barren garden of memory, unable to forget.

CHAPTER 8

KATIA

Katia is such an important part of my own Russian story that I must give her a chapter of her own. She provided my transition from the Soviet Union to the new Russia and has been with me from the beginning to the present. Most of what I know about Russia today I learned from Katia, her family, and her many friends and colleagues throughout the country.

Katia Genieva (photo sent to Marianna by Katia for this book)

I didn't know it then, but that trip to Moscow in October 1991, when I first spoke publicly about censorship and forged my partnership with Katia, was my final trip to the Soviet Union. When I returned four months later, in February 1992, my plane landed in Russia—not the republic but the country.

Katia met me at Sheremetevo International Airport, just outside passport control, which was highly irregular: in Soviet times only VIPs were met in this fashion, and I certainly wasn't a VIP. I was quaking in my warm winter boots, anticipating a hard time at the hands of the authorities, surely tipped off by my internal Soviet censor that Katia and I were up to no good on this visit. After all, we were plotting nothing less than an exhibition and scholarly conference on censorship in Russia and the Soviet Union; there were bound to be documents displayed and discussed that were critical of the government. Why let me in at all at this crucial time?

True, I had noticed a new mood even before we landed: for the first time in my experience, passengers didn't have to fill out forms listing every bit of money we were carrying in any currency or gold and silver jewelry we were wearing. We were not asked the usual international questions about drugs, weapons, and the purely Soviet question about whether we were bringing in "books and magazines for Soviet people." But I was still skittish and amazed to see Katia so soon after landing. She whisked me through customs, waving imperiously at the bored officers lounging at their "Nothing to Declare" counters marked by green lights.

We were driven into the city by Kolia, a Chernobyl victim Katia had hired to drive for the library. He dropped us at Katia's building and carried my large, heavy suitcase filled with gifts and necessities up to the fifth floor. As long as I've been visiting Katia in either of her flats, it has bothered me that someone had to carry my luggage up all those stairs. My suitcases were always large, always heavy. Katia insisted that the drivers were strong, and I never saw or heard any indication that they felt put upon. But after my first visit, I always brought little gifts for them: packs of Marlboros in the early 1990s, when this particular brand of American cigarettes was more valuable than any currency, and American music or chocolates later, after life had normalized a little.

Upstairs, Katia unlocked the heavy door and ushered me into the cozy flat, a major contrast to the dismal hallway. Iura, Dasha, Galina Pavlovna, and Mordash, the Irish terrier, embraced me like a long-lost family member. I was exhausted—jet lag plus the usual load of emotions I carried with me to Russia—but I was exhilarated as I had never been before upon arrival. I felt that I had truly launched on a professional and personal adventure of unimaginable magnitude. Moreover, I had a home and family to wake up to in the mornings and return to in the evenings. No more lonely, uncomfortable, troubling hotel rooms. Good-bye, Academy of Sciences Hotel, where I had counted roaches making their way up and down the bathroom walls in the 1980s! Farewell, Hotel Rossiia of the ill-fitting windows and frustrating hunts for breakfast! Most important, I had Katia as a companion now, guiding me on this amazing journey through the new Russia.

Katia and I met in July 1990. I had spent a week in Harrogate, England, a charming town filled with scholars from all over the world gathered for the Fourth World Congress on Soviet and East European Studies. I was one of the organizers of panels on library and bibliographic matters and the moderator of an informal discussion group on censorship. By now my passion for censorship issues had become quite well known in the Slavic studies community; one British historian referred to me as "Madame Censorship," a title I rather liked.

Scheduled at the same time as my discussion group was an information session on changes in Soviet libraries chaired by one Ekaterina Iur'evna Genieva. I'd never met her, but Emily Tall, a mutual American friend who shared Katia's scholarly interest in James Joyce, had told me that I really must meet "Katia," as everyone called her; we had so much in common, she assured me. So after our sessions, Katia and I met for coffee and immediately hit it off. She had just come through a dramatic election where she worked, at the Library for Foreign Literature, or Inostranka, as it's called, short for *inostrannaia*, foreign. Leninka, Inostranka, Publichka. The Russian language is rich in diminutives, and people, beloved libraries, and even water and cheese are given affectionate nicknames.

In the glasnost period, institutions had to elect their directors, and the Inostranka had replaced its former director, Liudmilla Kosygina, daughter of Aleksei Kosygin, one of the Soviet premiers, with Viacheslav Ivanov, a prominent philologist and son of Soviet writer Vsevolod Ivanov. Katia was elected deputy director and was running the library for Ivanov, who was busy with his scholarship and newly permitted travels abroad.

Katia is a tall, statuesque woman with thick, curly brown hair cut short, a warm smile, and glasses covering penetrating eyes that miss very little. Our eyes met, and although we didn't know it then, over the years we would turn out to be sister-friends. Her Russian was beautiful, with some unusual French touches here and there, contributions from her French-speaking maternal grandmother, whom she adored and who raised her during her mother's travels as a doctor. "Minor Russian nobility," Katia characterized her mother's family.

Her father, a Jew, was trained as a chemist and worked briefly at his profession, but he really wanted to be an actor and worked as one during World War II. After the war, he held management positions in several commercial institutions but was arrested in the late 1940s or early 1950s and served time in prison. Was he a victim of Stalin's anti-Jewish campaign? Katia doesn't know, but she told me that when he was released, a judge told him that had he lived in the United States, they might have built a monument to him.

Katia's parents divorced when she was an infant, and although she was raised by her mother's family, she remained in close touch with her father and his second wife for the rest of their lives. She also stayed close to their daughter Masha, her half-sister, and Tony, Masha's Italian-businessman husband.

Katia's maternal grandfather was a distinguished professor of civil engineering with the rank of a general who did some consulting for Stalin. Katia recalls that a little suitcase always stood by the door. She wanted to play with it but wasn't allowed to even touch it. When she was older, she grew to understand that the suitcase was there in case there was a knock on the door one night, as was so common in those immediate postwar years when Stalin was at his paranoid worst.

Her grandmother instilled in her a love for Russian Orthodoxy, but Katia also honored and felt a deep sympathy for her Jewish heritage and was therefore interested in my own background and practices. Through Katia I met progressive priests determined to liberalize the church and move it out of its Soviet phase. Before 1917, the Orthodox Church was tied closely to the state, and the vast majority of Russians were Orthodox Christians. When the Bolsheviks came to power and religion was declared "the opiate of the masses," the Orthodox Church, along with all other organized religions, was persecuted: churches were desecrated or destroyed, priests were sent to the gulag, wealth was nationalized, and the patriarch was made subject to the Communist leadership.

During glasnost the Orthodox Church began to rise again. Not so other religions, however, which the church viewed with suspicion. As the church began to regain its status, close to the ruling power, much of its wealth returned and troubling things started to happen. There was the brutal 1990 murder of Father Aleksandr Men, almost certainly committed by the KGB. Father Aleksandr, who was twelve years older than Katia, was a close family friend whom she remembers from earliest childhood. He was her spiritual father, and years later, when her husband, Iura, converted from Judaism to Christianity, Father Aleksandr baptized him. When I spend time with Katia, I always feel that Father Aleksandr is somewhere nearby and that we have an affinity for one another. I've been in his church and his house often, looked

A marker at the spot where Father Aleksandr Men was murdered

at the hundreds of books in many languages in his study, and spent time with his wife and son. I've stood at the spot where he was murdered as well as at his grave, covered in all seasons with fresh flowers.

Father Aleksandr had been born Jewish but was baptized in infancy by his mother, a convert. Like Katia, he respected his Jewish heritage and believed deeply in ecumenism. He lectured to great crowds in Katia's library and wrote well-regarded books.

In addition to speaking beautiful Russian, Katia had an extraordinary command of English, a lightly accented British English. Meeting her for the first time, one would think she had spent considerable time in the United Kingdom. Not so: her first trip was not until April 1975, when she was invited to be part of a delegation of young literary critics. Her host was John Roberts, then head of the Great Britain-USSR Association and later a close friend and colleague of Katia's and, eventually, mine.

Katia received an advanced degree in 1972 from Moscow State University with a dissertation on James Joyce's *Ulysses*, a topic unheard of for a Soviet student. She had to defend her dissertation twice, first before her department and then before a special commission. In the end her professors passed her, despite a warning from one that it would never happen while he was alive. She was told that she would never work in this field; Katia often does impossible things.

After meeting her, I invited Katia to visit in Urbana the following summer as a participant in the Summer Research Laboratory. During that time she became a fast friend of our family and an enthusiastic supporter of my research on imperial Russian censorship. Standing in my office on the first day of her visit, Katia studied the framed poster on my wall publicizing an exhibition I had curated for the New York Public Library in 1984, "Censorship in the Slavic World." As she studied the poster, I could practically see on her expressive face a daring idea forming.

"Let's prepare a censorship exhibition together," she proposed, with a sparkle in her eye. "We'll mount it in my library and then travel with it around the country!"

"But Katia," I recall demurring, "won't this be dangerous for you?"

"Maybe a little," she replied, "but I'm not afraid. I've already mounted exhibitions on anti-Semitism and other unpopular subjects, and here I am!"

Thus began our partnership, certainly the most important development in my professional life from that moment on. Additionally, we become the closest of friends. I'm an honorary member of Katia's family and she of mine.

Starting with that first post-Soviet trip in February 1992, I almost always stayed with Katia and her family, shoehorned into their fifth-floor walk-up outside the city center along with Iura; their daughter, Dasha; and Galina Pavlovna, Katia's godmother. I always brought Galina her favorite chocolates and talked with her about ballet, which we sometimes watched together on television. Galina Pavlovna had trained as a ballerina and would have had a fine career were it not for a freak accident: during her debut performance at the Bolshoi, her partner dropped her, and her injuries prevented her from ever dancing again. She never married but devoted herself to Katia, whom she and Katia's grandmother raised while Katia's doctor-mother was working.

Iura and one of the Mordashes at the dacha

Also in the family was Mordash, the Irish terrier who, when he died, was replaced by an identical Mordash. I've never been a fan of large dogs, so of course these two adored me and never let me out of their sight, to the family's great amusement.

The flat was a typical one of its period, in a *Khrushchevka*, a five-story building erected in the 1960s under Khrushchev and set on a large campus amidst many others, with a Metro stop nearby. Five-story buildings didn't qualify for elevators, which made this model popular and cheaper to erect. Although physically sound enough, the buildings were not in good condition, and despite the trees, playgrounds, and green spaces, they stood out: sorry heaps of various sizes with peeling paint, balconies strung with laundry, and dark, foul-smelling stairwells.

Buildings and neighborhoods like this one are ubiquitous in Soviet cities and their ideological offspring around the world. When I spot them in countries throughout Eastern Europe and in China, I feel at home, in a heart-sinking and unhappy sort of way. These housing developments, often stretching as far as the eye can see, are blisters on some otherwise attractive landscapes, and the images they bring to my mind remain bittersweet, reminding me of friendship and warmth inside their shabby exteriors.

Inside the heavy door (padded for extra warmth) of Katia's flat was a living room–dining room that also served as Katia's and Iura's bedroom. Two small bedrooms were for Galina Pavlovna and Dasha. The bathtub and sink were in one little room, the toilet in another, just as in many German apartments. Heavy furniture in good, dark wood—family pieces, some from before the revolution—dominated the too-small space. Books were crammed two deep into shelves, and the top of the old upright piano, covered with a lace doily, served as a surface for more books. Where there were no shelves, the walls and all available surfaces were covered with photos and portraits: relatives past and present, Father Aleksandr Men, and icons in their corner, as is traditional in an Orthodox home.

From my first moment in the flat that February, I was surrounded by warmth and affection, good kitchen smells such as cabbage (detested by many but loved by me), and animated voices. In all seasons we removed our boots or shoes at the door when we entered, exchanging them for *tapochki,* or backless slippers. In winter, Iura brushed away the snow and mud from our boots and coats. We ate hot *borshch* with heavenly black bread, dense and faintly sweet; cabbage salad; and boiled potatoes. We drank endless cups of tea, accompanied by chocolates from the Red October factory located right in the center of Moscow, on the Moskva River. In post-Soviet Russia we ate cold *borshch* in warm weather, more cabbage and potatoes, and the same wonderful bread, now accompanied by fresh herbs and fruits from shops and markets supplied by sellers from Azerbaijan, by then an independent country rather than one of the fifteen Soviet republics.

I usually slept poorly in Moscow, especially for the first week after flying, thanks to jet lag and excitement. In the early mornings during my winter visits, I lay in bed and listened to the muted sounds of shovels attacking the heaps of new snow. Each window consisted of two windows, with space between, an effective antidote to drafts in that frigid climate. The windows had *fortochki* too, little ventilation windows that opened independently in case you felt the need, in winter, for a little fresh air when the heating was too effective, or in summer when the stuffiness became unbearable. (No air conditioning in this northern climate.) In the winter, the sun didn't rise for hours, until well into the morning, and set by midafternoon.

In spring and summer the sun was with us well into the evening, and sunrise came early. In that brighter season I lay awake in the half-light of late evening and early morning and listened to birds sing in place of snow shovels. Breakfast was usually black bread, butter, maybe some thick Russian honey, cheese, perhaps kefir and curds, and occasionally juice. Now and then we ate kasha (buckwheat groats), the Russian equivalent of oatmeal, cooked with lots of butter. All these products came from different parts of Russia; very few products arrived from Europe.

Over the months, as Russia Westernized, however, I watched our meals change. State-owned shops now had competition—a totally new concept—from private enterprises, and their shiny shelves stocked up with imported goods. Yogurt, sausage, and cheeses from Germany and preserves from Israel. Local Russian food, particularly vegetarian items, disappeared almost totally in the early 1990s. The manufacturing and distribution systems fell apart along with the country, and practically everything started becoming imported. Meat and fish were usually available, although perhaps not of the highest quality or in wide variety.

But little by little, certainly by the mid-1990s, Russian food began to come back, and when Katia or Iura took me shopping, we could once again choose Russian yogurt, Russian jam, and Russian milk. It wasn't so much the taste of Russian products that I welcomed; rather, it was the evidence that the country was normalizing and beginning to feed its citizens. Black bread, that incomparable food, never really disappeared, although the price did rise.

Dasha, Katia's and Iura's only child, was sixteen when we first met in 1991. She was a beautiful girl, intense and rather moody, as girls her age everywhere can be. She was an artist, and when I told Harvey, he began packing in my suitcases art supplies unavailable in Moscow: paints, brushes, colored pencils, and tablets of drawing paper for the customs officers to paw through, if they ever chose to do so. In the Soviet economy, consumer goods had always been scarce and erratic. Men's socks, for example: I'll never forget a shopping trip in 1987, when an American colleague's suitcase failed to arrive in Moscow and we made an emergency run to a state clothing store; during this time all stores were state owned, with no private business permitted. We found men's socks, but only extra-large, woolly, stiff, and a sickly shade of greenish-yellow. My colleague decided to borrow socks from another man in our group instead.

In 2001, when she was twenty-five, Dasha married Andrei, a historian and publisher of highly respected books and archival material dealing with the Soviet Union's past and Russia's present and future. His series on Stalinism and on the gulag was impressive. By the time Andrei and Dasha married, I'd known him for several years, and I observed their courtship with pleasure. Andrei is a lovely, gentle man who seemed to me to view his high-powered mother-in-law with a slightly bemused fondness. I feel close to him both as a colleague and as a member of Katia's family.

In 2001 Katia and Iura moved to a spacious—by Soviet standards—apartment in the center of Moscow, with two full bathrooms and an elevator. Three years later Dasha and Andrei bought a smaller apartment in the same group of buildings. In May 2004 their son, Dania, was born, and Katia and I shared another bond as we became grandmothers in 2004. Back in the United States, Kate and Mary had given birth to Jessie and Cooper, respectively, only a few weeks apart.

The new flat was a joy. Iura, who is a construction expert, had renovated it completely, but I saw it for the first time when it was empty and unimproved. This part of central Moscow was lovely and quite different from their old neighborhood—urban, with older, pre-Soviet buildings, and I ran from one room to another with my camera to document for Harvey the window views of a cityscape with trees. From the study window was "the Rostovs' house," from *War and Peace*, with a monument to Tolstoy in the yard. From the kitchen and master bedroom windows the embassies of Germany and New Zealand were visible. Nearby was Tchaikovsky's house, now a "house-museum," and down the block stood the Soviet Writers' Union, in whose charming café we often ate. Across the street was an excellent Georgian restaurant that was the intriguing scene of a mafia-style murder. Finally, the neighborhood boasted the Foreign Ministry building, one of Stalin's seven "wedding-cake" skyscrapers. Iura's father, a builder, had worked on the Moscow State University skyscraper in the Lenin Hills section of the city.

Katia showed me their bedroom, with an en suite bathroom, and Galina Pavlovna's bedroom, with another bathroom next to it. The apartment included a gracious living room–dining room, a study that could double as a guest room, and a large kitchen with cheerful red cupboards and room for a full-sized refrigerator instead of the small one in their previous apartment. The best part was the elevator. Although only on the third floor, it was especially nice to have an elevator so a driver wouldn't have to drag my giant, overloaded suitcase up flights of stairs.

Katia and her family moved into the new flat in 2000, and when I came, we no longer felt cramped, although the space filled up quickly.

A steady stream of books flowed in, crowding the shelves, and their furniture looked elegant in the new flat now that there was more room. When I lay in bed, I still listened to the snow shoveling and the birds but also to the faint sound of someone practicing Chopin and Tchaikovsky on the piano. I soon began bringing my own music, and Katia always had the old upright tuned for me, so I could practice too. I tried not to compare myself to the invisible pianist who played far better than I do.

Russian Orthodox homes usually have an icon corner or home altar in the east corner of a room. In Katia and Iura's, in addition to the icon corner, there were photos of Father Aleksandr, as well as old family portraits from

Katia's mother's side—the "minor Russian nobility"—and recent pictures from Dasha's wedding and Katia's many activities. I enjoyed looking at them all and took special pleasure from some very nice photos of Katia with George Soros, one of the most talented and successful financiers the world has known. I knew him as the Hungarian-American philanthropist who, through his Open Society Institute-Russia, of which Katia was president, was transforming post-Soviet Russia and the rest of the region. Katia and I served together on the international board managing Soros's library program, revitalizing libraries throughout the former Communist world, bringing them into the worldwide library community, and, most important, making them available to their own communities. In my view, there has never been a philanthropist like George Soros, and perhaps there never will be again.

Katia's new home was in a historically interesting building, as is true of many in central Moscow. Along with embassy personnel, some well-known Soviet personalities lived in the complex, including Sergei Mikhalkov, who wrote and rewrote the lyrics to the Soviet national anthem at least three times between 1942 and 2001, to conform to the demands of different eras. During my February 2009 visit, Iura told me that President Putin had come the preceding March to Mikhalkov's apartment to wish him a happy ninety-fifth birthday. (Mikhalkov died a few months later.) His son, Nikita Mikhalkov, is a prominent Russian filmmaker and actor who now works in the United States as well as in Russia.

Some "new Russians," a derogatory term used to describe those who profited, often grandly, from the chaos accompanying the collapse of the Soviet Union, had bought apartments in the building complex, too. In Soviet times there were no rich people in the Western sense of the word. You might, however, be powerful through Communist Party connections, with perks that enabled you to live better than the average citizen, access to special stores with imported goods, and the ability to travel abroad. But after the collapse, when the country was in a chaotic transition to a market economy and there was essentially no legal system in place, the situation changed dramatically. Some people, often young party members with connections and strong entrepreneurial skills, were able to buy up state property and become billionaires. Soon a small number of rich people owned ostentatious houses and yachts and designer clothes and took frequent trips to the Riviera. Katia's new neighbors included some of those new Russian multimillionaires.

Wonderful as the new flat was, the family preferred the dacha Katia had inherited from her grandmother.

It is located in a community near Abramtsevo, the community established for academicians, artists, and writers and where my friend Galia Levina's family dacha is also located. After my first visit I understood why people yearn for their dachas: so many of the apartments in the city are small, cramped, and dark, with dirty, smelly hallways and staircases. Dachas, on the other hand, are built in forests of birch and pine, so the air is fresh. In winter, the snow is clean and white; in summer gardens of vegetables and flowers flourish, and birds sing. Some dachas are small, primitive, and not winterized, but Katia's and Galia's are both suitable for year-round living. Iura, an accomplished builder, maintained their dacha splendidly. When I first visited, there was only an outhouse and detached shower house, but over the years Iura had installed indoor plumbing and made other improvements.

Katia and Iura outside the dacha

Katia and Iura at the dining room table in the dacha

Eventually, he built two more dachas on the grounds, one for Dasha and family and one to serve as a guesthouse.

The dacha village was recently threatened by a new road, in a vain attempt to deal with the impossible traffic in the area surrounding Moscow. Soon dachas may be gone, which would be a great loss. Katia spent much of her childhood there, with her grandmother, sheltered from Soviet life, while Dasha, too, considers theirs to be her "real" home, spending time there with Dania. I too came to love dacha culture. I slept better there than in Moscow, and Katia and I had some of our best brainstorming sessions while preparing lunch, washing dishes, or having tea and jam at the round wooden table that could be expanded to seat a dozen. In winter we worked at the table, while clean white snow drifted against the windows; in summer we sat outside on the porch drinking our tea and enjoying the fresh greenery as we worked. How sad it would be to lose the dacha if that road did come through.

Soon Katia and I took our censorship exhibitions on the road within Russia and other countries of the former Soviet Union. Later, Katia came to the United States, and we gave talks together at the American Library Association and the American Association for the Advancement of Slavic Studies.

She stayed with us in Champaign, visited Chicago, and met our daughters, Kate and Mary. In June 1996, Harvey and the girls accompanied me to Russia, and afterward the girls prepared a document titled "Rules for Marianna and Katia." In a somewhat comical attempt to control the two of us, the list of rules sought to curtail our travels and communication and addressed our use of cells, pagers, and e-mail to discuss our upcoming travels and exhibits concerning censorship. The girls signed and dated the list to make it legally binding, and we put green marbled frames around two originals, one for Katia and one for me. My copy is in my study at home; hers is in her office at the Library for Foreign Literature. We glance at them occasionally from opposite sides of the world and smile.

CHAPTER 9

GALINA PAVLOVNA'S FUNERAL AND MORE THOUGHTS ON RELIGION

Istopped in to see Galina Pavlovna when I arrived at Katia's flat on a Thursday night in June 2003. She had been failing for some time, and I prepared myself as I entered her room. She was in a comatose state, breathing heavily, and her condition reminded me vividly of Mama's in the last days of her life, four years earlier. I felt that familiar tightening in my throat, the accelerated beating of my heart, the hard knot in my stomach; I wondered whether she'd make it through the night. But I was glad Galina Pavlovna could die at home, in her own bed. Mama could not; she had had dementia and spent her final years in a nursing home, a good place where she was content. She died one cold April day. Harvey, Kate, Mary, and I had just visited. We had gone for a meal at an Indian restaurant nearby when the call came.

Papa had also been in the nursing home but only for two months, in and out of dementia by then. But he never lost his energy and determination; several times he attempted to walk out of the home, overcoat on, briefcase in hand, to attend an imagined meeting or a demonstration. Once he lay down in front of the fourth-floor elevator in a silent, peaceful demonstration. He died peacefully one January night in 1995.

These were the memories that flooded my mind as I lay in bed that night, waiting for sleep to come. At the suggestion of one of my doctors, I tried Ambien that first night in Moscow to combat jet lag and slept through the hubbub when Galina Pavlovna's death was discovered. The next days were devoted to funeral preparations, which I studied as I knew Papa would want me to, writing down every detail. I had been in Orthodox churches during funerals but had never been involved in one personally, so there was much to take in.

On Saturday, the day before the funeral, Katia and I went with Andrei and Dasha to the morgue, now a privately run funeral home. Previously it had been a hospital for the Central Committee elite. We brought wreaths and flower arrangements that Katia had ordered the day before from the florist. Now Katia and Dasha arranged the flowers around Galina Pavlovna's head and covered her lower body with them. She wore a familiar dress, a kerchief tied loosely over her hair. Beside the coffin, Dasha wept bitterly. Galina Pavlovna had been a grandmother to her. I knew how she felt: my maternal grandma had lived with us too, part of the intimate family circle in which I grew up. It's so difficult to experience these rituals for the first time, the loss of someone you've known and loved and whose presence you've taken for granted all your life, and hovering over you is the realization that your parents will be next. I held Dasha's hand, gave her tissues, and murmured words that I hoped would be reassuring as the coffin was closed and we rode to the church behind the minibus that served as a hearse. Galina Pavlovna spent this night, before her funeral, in the church.

The next day, Sunday, we came early to Saints Cosmas and Damian Church. It was a beautiful sunny day, and the cool interior of the church welcomed us. There were a few chairs for those who needed them, and Katia encouraged me to sit and watch. At a little past 11 a.m., the regular mass concluded, and worshippers had a snack. Katia brought me a first-rate bagel to share, a real bagel, such as I haven't tasted in the United States since childhood. (Bagels, which probably originated in Jewish Eastern Europe, used to be, and in Russia still are, small and dense, something to sink your teeth into. The large, soft rolls we call bagels in America do not resemble them, except for the doughnut shape.)

Two funerals were taking place simultaneously, though we didn't know the man whose coffin lay near Galina Pavlovna's. Nevertheless, some men, family members or fellow parishioners, moved the two coffins to the center of the church in front of the altar, and Father Georgii and Father Aleksandr Borisov presided. The two priests chanted the funeral mass, accompanied by a small choir. Galina Pavlovna's coffin was open, and her few relations, Katia's family, coworkers, and her friends filed past by the coffin, each kneeling to kiss her forehead and say a few words. Katia went first, showing her deep love and respect by prostrating herself three times. When the mass was over, Father Georgii sprinkled earth over her body and read from a paper placed on her chest and forehead a prayer absolving her sins. A young priest, now in street clothes, nailed the coffin shut, and we followed Father Georgii, leading the pallbearers out of the church.

The burial was in Vagankovskoe Cemetery, a place I'd wanted to visit for years because Vladimir Vysotskii is buried there. You can't miss his tomb, marked by a large, gilded statue and always covered with flowers. Vysotskii was an actor, singer, poet, and songwriter who soared across the Russian cultural scene of the 1960s and 1970s before crashing in 1980 at age forty-two, done in by drugs, alcohol, and, I venture to guess, disgust with the Soviet state. He was enormously popular in life and in death, and his ghost is everywhere.

Vysotskii's was not by any means the only grave I wanted to see in Vagankovskoe Cemetery. Vladimir Dal' lies there, the great lexicographer of the nineteenth century whose work looms over all scholars in Russian studies and whose great dictionary I often consulted. Bulat Okudzhava is buried there too, another enormously influential balladeer and poet a few years senior to Vysotskii but fortunate enough to outlive the Soviet Union. Last, but certainly not least in my imagination, is Sergei Esenin, writer of some of the most beautiful lyric poetry in Russian, most of it banned until the mid-1960s. Dead by his own hand in 1925 at the age of thirty, he was also the onetime husband of the great American dancer Isadora Duncan.

In Vagankovskoe there's much to contemplate, but that day we came to bury a good and much-loved family member. Galina Pavlovna's coffin was lowered into the grave, which was then filled in with the reddish dirt. Each of us dropped a handful of soil onto the coffin—I'm familiar with this part of the ritual, since we Jews do something similar—and green fronds were laid over that, followed by a layer of flowers. Finally, they placed a large oak cross atop the grave and in a year would erect a proper tombstone just as we do in the Jewish tradition. Were there any Jewish graves at Vagankovskoe, with Hebrew writing on the tombstones and Stars of David? Katya said there were quite a few Jews buried there, including some members of her father's family. While Jews were not welcome in Soviet times, now it is routine.

Standing at Galina Pavlovna's grave on a beautiful summer day, I returned to my persistent thoughts about religion in Russia. I'm always aware of Katia's spirituality and deep devotion to her religion, but I feel it especially at the dacha, not far from the little church where Father Aleksandr Men presided and is buried, a short distance from the spot where he was cut down with an ax by a supposedly unknown assailant. The aura is strong too in the Moscow flat. It's not just the icons in both homes or the photos of Father Aleksandr Men. If it were only that, I might feel excluded. But this is an aura that envelops me, an American Jew, too, and not just in Katia's two homes. I don't go in for auras in Chicago, but I definitely feel the presence of spirituality in Russia, and it affects me deeply.

When I'm in Russia, especially with Katia, I find myself thinking a great deal about Orthodoxy and Judaism. Orthodoxy has been the dominant religion in Russia during the twenty-first century and had been from its introduction into Russia in the ninth century. I had read about Russian Orthodoxy in college and graduate school, but when I began staying with Katia's family, the religion came to life for me. I saw how they observed its rituals and their emotional attachment to them. I began to pay more attention to Russian Orthodox churches, beautiful structures with gilded onion domes and brightly painted exteriors. During the Soviet years, when religion was officially out of favor, churches were used as warehouses, neglected, or destroyed. Katia's church, Saints Cosmas and Damian, was protected because it housed the Library for Foreign Literature in the 1920s; Katya had a plaque placed on the building: "This church saved books."

Father Aleksandr Borisov and Father Georgii, progressive priests and close friends of Katia's, serve in this historic little sixteenth-century church in the center of Moscow. Father Georgii became a good friend of mine as well, but he unfortunately died of cancer in 2008. A slight man who moved and talked quickly, he was head of the Religious Department in Katia's library. As far as I know, this was the first such department in a post-Soviet Russian library with collections and reference works on religions of the world that was open to everyone. The Orthodox establishment is not particularly liberal or progressive, and there is a supernationalistic wing that troubles my

Orthodox friends, who work tirelessly to move the church away from that extreme. (I sense that it's something of an uphill battle.)

I'd seen many sad churches around Russia, with doors hanging askew, paint faded, and domes stripped of their gilt. But since the early 1990s, many churches were now working again, their gilt and paint restored; priests, monks, and nuns in attendance; and growing numbers of worshippers attending mass. Some families, like Katia's, had never given up their religion, but many put it aside out of fear. Untold numbers of believers were executed in cellars and buried in mass graves or languished in the gulag. But seventy years is a long time, and people who want to rediscover their Orthodoxy must learn everything anew.

When I peeked into churches during Soviet times, I would see only a few old women inside, dark shawls covering their heads and shoulders. During glasnost, in the late 1980s, the old women were still there, but there had been a sea change. The television showed prominent people such as entertainers and even Communist Party leaders entering churches to have their children baptized or become baptized themselves. Men and women wore visible crosses around their necks for all to see. People discussed baptism, and weddings began taking place in church, where brides wore long white dresses and veils, grooms wore dark suits, and the ceremony was performed by a party official with all due pomp. Friends say that some of the current religiosity is just for show, that being Orthodox is "in." But clearly some people are sincere and are connecting, or reconnecting, with their spiritual selves and their centuries-old traditions.

I was beginning to adjust to this change in Soviet life, along with so many others, but each time I landed in the country, I was bowled over by something new. In June 1988, with glasnost still the Soviet Union, I arrived in Moscow from Beijing, bleary-eyed from eight hours in a smoke-filled plane, and disembarked to find the arrivals hall filled with religious dignitaries from all over the world milling around, garbed in colorful robes and headdresses. I'd forgotten that my visit coincided with the celebrations marking the millennium of Christianity in Russia; all week the media were filled with ceremonies and rituals. Was Lenin, who followed Marx in denouncing religion, turning over in his mausoleum in Red Square? If so, it must happen during the night, when the ever-popular tourist site is closed. It is an image that I enjoy.

There is a charming legend about how Grand Prince Vladimir of Kiev (then the hub of the Russian state) a millennium ago chose Christianity for his people. He is said to have sent envoys to view the rites of neighboring religions. The envoys rejected Islam for, among other reasons, its ban on alcoholic beverages. Judaism was unacceptable because the Jews had lost Jerusalem: clearly, God must have abandoned them. German-style Christianity struck them as too gloomy and joyless. But the Byzantine ritual at Hagia Sophia in Constantinople overwhelmed them with its beauty, and thus did Orthodox Christianity come to Russia. Vladimir had the population of Kiev baptized in the River Dnieper, and the roots of what was to become state religion for the next millennium—with a decided bend in the tree for seventy years in the twentieth century—took hold.

I've come to love the inside of Orthodox churches. As I travel around Russia in the twenty-first century, I see younger men and women in churches and lots of children. The soaring space is dim and cool in summer and warm and welcoming in winter. There are no pews. Worshippers stand facing the iconostasis (icon stand), which is a wall of paintings that separates the nave from the sanctuary. Only priests may enter the altar area. The smells of incense and burning candles pervade the air, and lines form for confession taken by several priests at small altars. The presiding priest and choir chant beautiful prayers in Old Church Slavonic, the Russian Orthodox equivalent of Latin.

The ambiance could not be more different from the synagogues of my tradition, and yet I feel at home there. Perhaps my familiarity and sense of comfort come from a shared spirituality. Sometimes when the anniversary of the death of one of my loved ones comes while I'm in Russia and Katia and I are near a church, we go in and I light a candle and I recite Kaddish, the Jewish prayer for the dead, while Katia lights a candle for her loved ones and says her Orthodox prayer. Traditional Jews would probably find this shocking; our tradition requires a minyan, ten Jewish men, to say Kaddish, and even with a minyan they certainly would not approve of saying Kaddish in a church. But I'm a Reform Jew who believes that women can and should be part of a minyan, and I believe, too, that my prayer will ascend wherever I am, even if I am alone. When I'm with Katia, our prayers ascend together, and that is as it should be.

We talk about our religions while sitting at the kitchen table. I'm always aware of my Judaism in ways that are sometimes pleasant, sometimes unpleasant, and always tinged with sadness. My grandparents had left the empire in a great wave of Jewish persecution around 1900. "A third of Jews will be converted, a third will emigrate, and the rest will die of hunger." The reactionary Russian statesman Konstantin Pobedonostsev may or may not have said these words, but the sentiment was certainly accurate in official circles during the reign of Tsar Alexander III, who presided over the mass exodus of Jews.

My family, Harvey's family, and the families of so many others came to America and made good lives. We were safe from the tsar and Pobedonostsev and safe, during World War II, from the Holocaust on Soviet soil. I was born in February 1942 in Chicago. Most of the Jewish children born in February 1942 in Zhitomir, my father's ancestral town, or in Uzda, where my mother's people lived, ended up in mass graves. In my mind's eye I see them. This vision has troubled me since I was old enough to know about the fate of European Jews, by the time I was about eight and long before I became connected to Russia. I used to talk to Papa about it, and he would look at me and quote, "There, but for the grace of God, go I."

As an adult I once read about a young Jewish partisan girl in Belarus (then the Belorussian Republic of the Soviet Union), perhaps not far from Uzda. Her name might have been Marianna (at least I wanted it to be), and she was caught, tortured, and executed by the Nazis in February 1942, the month and year of my birth. The coincidences overwhelmed me, and I've always identified with that brave, martyred girl who died a terrible and heroic death just when I, another Jewish girl with roots close to hers, was born in Chicago. She died; I was born into safety. Whenever I recite Kaddish, she is in my thoughts. Whenever I am in Russia, she is in my thoughts, somewhere at the back of my consciousness.

Isaac Neuman, my late rabbi in Champaign, a survivor of several camps, including Auschwitz, was surprised when I told him that I considered myself a survivor too—not like him, of course, but a survivor nonetheless because I was born in Chicago and not in Uzda or Zhitomir. He respected my view, for which I'm grateful.

What about the Jews who stayed in Russia? So many of my Russian friends are Jews, or half Jews, or former Jews who weren't able or chose not to emigrate to Israel, the United States, or elsewhere. Their stories and lives engage me deeply; I have an ongoing conversation with myself about them. In Russia I see Jews in an entirely different light. Their faces look like my family's, but how wide the gap between me and them! We lived on different planets, of course, and that abyss separated us sharply: I grew up with ease and they with indescribable hardship. I can't stop thinking about them and wondering: What does our common heritage count for? By accident of fate—by the grace of God, if you will—are we now too far apart to be Jews together?

When I'm in Russia, I'm surrounded by those people I love or am fond of who are half Jewish, half Orthodox, like Katia and her colleague Zhenia or Father Aleksandr Men, whom I didn't know but whose presence I feel near me. Katia and Zhenia had Jewish fathers and Orthodox mothers and were raised Orthodox but love and respect their Jewish halves. It's clear to me that this is real and deep: their fathers' culture is an important part of who they are, and they see nothing odd about it. Zhenia told me about her father, an actor in the Moscow State Jewish Theater founded in 1919 and closed by the Soviet authorities in 1948. Its shining star was the actor Solomon Mikhoels, a brilliant actor murdered on Stalin's orders in 1948, his body run over to make his death seem like a car accident. Zhenia's father was a young actor in the company when the troubles began, and he lay low and survived.

A few of my Russian friends converted to Russian Orthodoxy, like Katia's husband Iura, whom I love like a brother-in-law. The rational part of me accepts conversion; I believe every individual should have the right to espouse any religion he or she chooses. At the same time, my emotional side is uncomfortable with conversion from Judaism to Christianity in countries with a strong state religion and a history of persecution of minority religions. I think about Benjamin Disraeli, Heinrich Heine, and Felix Mendelssohn, to mention a few non-Russians, and wonder what was going on in their heads and in their hearts when they converted. Were they genuinely drawn to Christianity? I'm sure the answer is yes, in many cases. Were they tired of anti-Semitism and living as persecuted outsiders and thus converted? The answer is probably also yes in many cases.

My feelings don't diminish my love for these good friends, but they do complicate my emotional life. I am drawn to my Russian-Jewish "family," but there is much I don't understand and can't come to grips with. Reform Jews like me were virtually unknown in Russia until the glasnost period. The Union for Reform Judaism in the United States describes Reform Jews as rooted in tradition but willing to introduce innovation, too. This describes me well.

These days there is a tiny Reform presence in Russia, mainly in Moscow and St. Petersburg. The Lubavitcher Jews, on the other hand, are everywhere Jews live in the former Soviet Union. An Orthodox Jewish Chasidic movement born in the Russian Empire in the eighteenth century, the Lubavitcher Jews are headquartered in Brooklyn and are active worldwide as well as in their ancestral home. Their members began streaming into the country during glasnost, to proselytize among their brothers and sisters in the Soviet Union and make "real" Jews out of them. In their eighteenth-century garments, Lubavitchers stand out wherever they are, while Reform Jews are indistinguishable from the general population.

As a Reform Jew, I have a problem with the Lubavitchers, and my feelings about this group cut especially close to home. As a good civil libertarian, I respect their right to practice their version of Judaism, but it is definitely not mine. How could I accept a form of Judaism that does not consider women to be equals in religious matters? Women are not permitted to read from the Torah with the men or to be counted in a minyan. I've never been able to abide this, and it pains me to see the Lubavitchers flooding Russia in recent years in the absence of an equally strong liberal presence to give Russian Jews options as they explore their Jewish identity. And yet I'm glad the Lubavitchers are there too, because they do good work. It's not simple for me.

Galina Pavlovna's funeral over, we leave the cemetery and drive to a restaurant called Pushkin, an elegant establishment that looks old but is new and serves delicious food with excellent service. When I dine at Pushkin, I can't help but think about that painful, hilarious family dinner at the Hotel Natsional in 1960, during my very first visit to Russia. There's absolutely no resemblance. Now the Natsional is a luxury hotel serving German business people, "new" Russians, and other guests with real money. How many people, I wonder, still remember the old Natsional? Does anyone miss it? Not I!

CHAPTER 10

MADAME CENSORSHIP HITS
THE ROAD

I came to post-Soviet Russia three times in 1992, and each time I was as anxious as ever about entering the country. Katia knew how I felt and met me at the airport in Moscow the first couple of times. She even sweet-talked the authorities into allowing her to enter the area where passengers collect their luggage before clearing customs. I felt tears coming, I was so relieved to see her. My internal Soviet censor was still functioning, and I knew what he was thinking: Marianna was up to no good here. Someone in charge needed to interrogate her, search her luggage, and take away her books, not to mention the children's clothing, giant bottles of aspirin and vitamins, condoms, and Barbie doll clothes. Open her purse, her passport case. How many dollars was she carrying? To whom would she give them? Who gave this anti-Soviet woman a visa? What an error! My Soviet censor knew those customs officers: they were his buddies. He watched Marianna waiting fearfully with resignation for them to approach her. But Katia was there, and the officials were no match for Katia. My censor always subsided at the last moment.

Katia was often there when I left the country, too, especially on my early trips. We didn't talk about it much, but I knew she sensed my terror. At the counter where you show your passport and begin the departure process, my censor would rear his head again and beckon to the customs officers: "Over here, fellows! Marianna is back! She's sneaking out subversive materials!" But the officers were indifferent to me, and Katia was there, so again my censor would back down. But on every subsequent trip he has curled up inside me, ready to lunge whenever I find myself in a Russian airport, entering or leaving the country.

As 1992 dawned, I became aware of a new internal voice, quite a stern, feminine one, which I came to think of as my American critic. I'd heard her voice from time to time over the past few months since the Mortenson Center, where we brought librarians from around the world to connect with each other and exchange ideas and practices, was established. But I was so busy getting our program started that I didn't pay much attention to her voice. Sometimes she perched on my shoulder like Pinocchio's Jiminy Cricket, an old friend. Hers was that annoying little voice that whispers in your ear when you forget something really big and important, and sometimes she really raked me over the coals. Our conversations went something like this:

"Who do you think you are?"

"I'm just trying to understand censorship in Russia and the Soviet Union," I'd reply.

"So you've learned a little something about that. Fine, but what about us Americans? Do you think we're perfect?"

"Of course not," I'd hasten to say. By now I responded defensively.

"Oh, give me a break! When you were a kid, you lived in a liberal bubble. Freedom of expression everywhere. Parents, teachers, librarians, the whole community: surely you don't think you Hyde Parkers were typical! You all actually thought that Adlai Stevenson would be our next president!"

"Yes, we did," I'd respond weakly.

"Aha!" she'd exclaim triumphantly. "What do you know about the real America?" "Well, I live here, don't I? I read *The New York Times* and *The New Yorker*, and I listen to NPR." I knew she was going to throttle me now.

"Oh my goodness," she would respond mockingly. "What on earth are you going to tell the Russians? You don't have a clue how things actually work *here*. You've spent all your time thinking about that other planet. You'd better get busy and learn what we on this planet are really like! Because they're going to ask you for guidance, you know, and you'd better have something useful to tell them!" And with a withering glance she would stomp off, muttering to herself.

Where did that voice come from? What was really bothering me? Maybe she was born of my underlying uneasiness about my attitude toward the Soviet Union. Had my focus on censorship, a dark topic, pushed me into a Cold War mentality that offended my liberal self? Papa was my model, and he certainly didn't paint the Soviet Union in stark black and white, as I had found myself doing. He had no love for the Soviets and their system, but he wanted to understand them on their own terms. He was a patriot in the best sense, meaning he loved our country and was its critic at the same time: he wanted us to do better. Why wasn't I listening more to Papa's voice?

She was right, of course, my sharp-tongued critic: I needed to educate myself and quickly. Because Russian colleagues, as well as librarians from other countries attending Mortenson Center programs, were indeed asking me for guidance. Many of them assumed that the United States, that land of milk and honey, had perfect freedom of the press: no censorship at all along its gold-paved streets. Of course, I knew this wasn't true and never had been. I was aware of the American Library Association's annual Banned Books Week, although I hadn't paid much attention to it, except to note that *The Adventures of Huckleberry Finn* was always in trouble in some public or school library. I certainly knew about the McCarthy-era blacklisting of writers, filmmakers, musicians. Pete Seeger, one of my family's favorite folk-singers, was on the list. And I remember buying a copy of D. H. Lawrence's *Lady Chatterley's Lover* in Paris in 1958 and smuggling it into the United States, where it was still banned, along with works by Henry Miller. Sex scared us Americans even more than politics. Bringing that book into the country illegally didn't bother me at all, by the way; I remember thinking how un-American it was to ban books, and I broke that law without a second thought. Was I on some FBI list? Probably!

I should have given myself a little credit for having begun to examine intellectual freedom issues in the United States in the mid-1980s, before I began hearing my American critic's voice. While I was writing the introduction to *Fence around the Empire*, I realized that I needed some American perspective, and with Harvey's and Papa's encouragement I asked an Urbana colleague in communications to recommend some books. I was stunned to discover a chilling passage on the power of television sponsors: apparently a gas company would not permit mention of gas chambers in a television play about the Holocaust.

I began to see patterns, but I didn't pursue them just then; I was too busy watching the Soviet Union self-destruct to think much about America. But by 1990–1991, I was definitely ready to think about us again. Librarians whom I had brought to the Mortenson Center from all over the world, and not just from Communist countries, knew that I studied censorship and was even considered an expert on the subject. They were beginning to ask about comparisons between their own countries and censorship in the United States. By this time my American critic was really leaning on me. Papa and Harvey, both much nicer than my critic, encouraged me to talk to colleagues who studied US history and culture for suggestions, and soon I was flooded with books to read.

By the early 1990s, I had learned quite a bit about censorship in the United States and was ready to try out my ideas on Russian audiences. I wanted to describe how I saw censorship issues in our country and what part of our experience might be useful to them in their emergence from omnicensorship. In addition to the exhibition and a speech I would give at the roundtable in Moscow, Katia was working with colleagues around the country to bring our exhibition to other Russian cities, and librarians in those cities were talking to university colleagues to create corresponding exhibitions of their own from their own archives. They would also plan roundtable discussions to take place while the exhibitions were on display, which I would speak at as well.

Here's my understanding of American "censorship," a word that remains in quotes because I remain unconvinced that it is the right term for what we do. Certainly what happens in our country is nothing like Soviet omnicensorship, nor, judging by my observations, is it like what goes on in most other countries.

Rising above us like the Statue of Liberty is the First Amendment to our Constitution, the revered opening of our Bill of Rights, guaranteeing, in historian Jill Lepore's succinct paraphrase, "the right to speak and to believe, and to write and to publish, freely."[1] The First Amendment arches over us, while below it, like a vast ocean, are the whitecaps and tsunamis of challenges to it. They bubble up from the bottom, disturbances created by every

---

1   Jill Lapore, "One Nation, under the Gun," *New Yorker*, April 23, 2012, online edition.

variety of civil-society group, each with its own issues of religion, race, ethnicity, gender, the environment, animal rights, smoking, alcohol, guns, and the like.

Each group aims to protect our citizens, especially children, from the dangerous, harmful, and "wrong" ideas expressed in printed works, on television and in the movies, on the Internet, in plays and exhibitions, and anywhere else ideas might lurk. These groups mount boycotts and demonstrations, and they remove books from libraries; this last occurs with great regularity. A school district or a public library board takes *Adventures of Huckleberry Finn* off the shelf, usually because it contains the word "nigger." Thanks to help from some organizations that take the First Amendment seriously, the removers of books are often taken to court, where they generally lose their cases, protected by the First Amendment looming above us and buttressed by those extremely vigilant civil-society organizations.

But the struggle never abates much, and the First Amendment is challenged continually. The US Supreme Court has heard a few such cases and has upheld the First Amendment. But what lies ahead?

I have no name for our kind of "censorship." I tend to think of it as "from-the-bottom-up challenges," which isn't very elegant. Our government, like all governments, does attempt some censorship of a traditional kind, mainly for military and national security issues. Traditionally, our citizens have given our government a hard time about such instances once we're made aware of them, usually by a whistle-blower who reveals information deemed harmful to our national interest. The "Pentagon Papers" is such a case from the Vietnam War era; the most prominent whistle-blower currently is Edward Snowden.

But it's the "bottom-up" variety that surrounds us and characterizes censorship in our daily lives. In recent years the Internet, social media, and cell phones have brought us to new heights and depths of complexity, providing both governments and interest groups much to be excited about. The news is filled with thought-provoking images these days: young people in the Middle East making revolutions, phones in hand; governments pressuring social media to close certain Internet sites to users in their countries. Meanwhile, religious and political conservatives continue to harangue libraries: books they disapprove of must go. We don't hear as much these days from feminist groups or others—conservatives seem to be front and center—but this can change; in our country it's difficult to predict what might come next.

Bringing censorship on the road was going to be the venue that would allow me to speak in Russia and in other countries about freedom of expression in my own country: bring on the audience! Through the 1990s and the first years of the new century, I did talk about these issues, and often with most of the six hundred librarians from seventy-six countries who came to the Mortenson Center during my tenure as Mortenson Professor and with librarians in the twenty-five or so countries that I visited. I gave talks in China, Colombia, Costa Rica, Germany, Guatemala, Haiti, Nicaragua, Salvador, Singapore, South Africa, and Vietnam. I talked in countries of Eastern Europe formerly in the Soviet sphere: Bulgaria, Croatia, Hungary, Macedonia, Poland, Romania, and Slovenia. I spoke in some of the newly minted countries of the former Soviet Union, such as Armenia, Estonia, Georgia, Kazakhstan, Latvia, Lithuania, Ukraine.

And, of course, I talked all over Russia, which helped me improve my message. My highly intelligent audiences kept me humble by asking good questions relaying the situation in their own countries. Sometimes they challenged my views, for which I was grateful because it allowed me to constantly refine my message. Sometimes—and these were my most interesting encounters—the audience remained quiet. Sitting impassively, they listened attentively but made no response. Then, at the end when it was time to leave, a few people approached me and spoke in low tones. I'd gotten it right, they whispered.

"Here's what happened to me."

"Do you think we could create civil society here in Russia?"

"Thank you for coming."

And I felt my American critic relax just a little bit.

I can recall only one hostile response during a presentation, and it came from an administrator. We were in Novosibirsk a few years ago, taking part in a winter cultural festival, and I gave the same talk twice, at a private humanities university and at the city's pedagogical university. The rector of the humanities university, a former Soviet military man, sat next to me on the platform as I spoke in Russian to an audience of students and faculty members.

I quoted Anatoly Kuznetsov on self-censorship and mentioned other writers who had been victims of omnicensorship. As I spoke, I was aware that, as usual, the students were right with me, but I could feel the rector growing more and more agitated. When I finished, he jumped in before anyone could ask a question and warned the audience not to pay any attention to what they had just heard. "The authors she talked about," he said disdainfully, "weren't our best writers. They were dissidents, people who left the country." Undeterred, a young female student raised her hand politely and shot right back: "But what about Solzhenitsyn? He's the best, isn't he? And he came back!"

I flew to Moscow six times between February 1992 and May 1993 to get the censorship exhibition ready, six weeks of long, very intense days of preparation. Katia and I sat in her pleasant kitchen every day over endless cups of tea early in the morning and late at night, planning. I never quite believed that this exhibition would actually happen—not because I didn't trust Katia but because I felt as though I were living in some kind of dream. When we left the flat, I found myself on the other planet, giddy from the constant changes under way out there, but inside, I was safe in the kitchen. My new family enveloped me. I peppered them with questions, and they tried to explain what I didn't understand. We watched television together, ate together, laughed together, woke up and fell asleep together.

This was the first time I'd lived with a family there, and I experienced with them the feel, the smell, the sound, and the taste of change. Breathtaking contrasts were everywhere: German yogurt and cheese, French wines and chocolates on the shelves of fancy shops a few steps from impromptu street markets where unsmiling, silent men and women spread their possessions on the ground, hoping to sell something. There were earrings, screwdrivers, hand-embroidered tablecloths, and encyclopedias. Little Soviet-made Ladas shared the streets with big, shiny BMWs. Women wrapped in heavy coats and shawls shared the sidewalks with stylish young things in designer leather and fur.

We left for the library each morning around eight. One of the library drivers picked us up outside Katia's block of flats, and we spent nearly an hour in the heavy traffic streaming into the city center. Katia and I sat in the backseat, she on her cell phone, I looking out the window. I listened as she arranged our lives for the coming day, confirming meetings, arranging special events for the library staff—meat deliveries and warm parkas from China to be sold in the building because there were none in the shops, manicures because there was no salon nearby—lining up transportation to and from an embassy reception. Lulled by my chronic jet lag, I watched the passing scene, now sharp, now fuzzy, depending on the weight of my eyelids. Small children walking with their babushkas (grandmothers) to school, boats on the Moscow River, streetcars overflowing with passengers.

As we approached the city center, the Kremlin loomed up before us, gold and white onion domes, massive red brick walls and towers. Moments from the library I spotted two landmarks I'd come to watch for: a jewel of a small church painted bright blue and one of Stalin's seven skyscrapers, a gigantic block of flats with shops around the base. Suddenly I was wide awake, alert with anticipation.

A moment later we pulled up in front of the Library for Foreign Literature, an unremarkable modern building that wouldn't appear out of place in any city. It was nearly empty at that time of day, and the broad street running along one side of the library was relatively quiet. During the day or in the evening, it's as much as your life is worth to venture across, but when I needed to, I would find a few natives and negotiate the street with them, a practice that has kept me safe in many countries. In the morning Katia and I have the place to ourselves, except for the night shift of cleaners and *militsia*, members of the Moscow police force hired to guard the library.

At home in Urbana, I'm used to arriving at my library between 7 and 8 a.m., so it feels luxurious to arrive much later. But most of Katia's staff leaves at 6 p.m., when it's been dark for hours during a Moscow winter, and she herself rarely leaves before 7 or 8 p.m., or even midnight. Exception: one of her two secretaries is always on duty as long as Katia is in the library, and two drivers (Katia doesn't drive) take turns ferrying her around Moscow to dinners or receptions at embassies and breakfasts with visiting European colleagues. There are concerts, often by students and teachers from the world-famous Moscow Conservatory; lectures by well-known academics and foreign visitors; exhibition openings; holiday children's parties; and many more events in the library as well, and Katia introduces most of them. The library also hosts fashion and craft shows highlighting the work of Russian artisans. Yes, long days and nights are nothing unusual.

We entered the library through a doorway with a large British Council sign affixed to it. This was new, Katia told me; David Whitwell, an English contractor, had renovated space for the British Council right here by the door, and now he was renovating many other areas within the library. I could still find traces of the old Soviet building—David couldn't work fast enough to cover them all up—but the library's appearance and functionality have changed radically from each of my visits to the next.

The BBC standing exhibition, with live TV and phones transmitting genuine English voices, is two floors up. (This is the installation for which Katia signed an agreement while the coup attempt was in progress.) On one of my visits in the early 1990s, the French Ministry of Foreign Affairs dedicated the elegant French Cultural Center in the library. Katia shared with me plans being developed with the US embassy for an American center in the library, a solid symbol of my country's cultural presence in Russia.

Katia greeted the cleaners and asked about their health and families. We walked past the podium where the *militsioner* sat and on up the stairs to the administrative suite at the top. David had created a tasteful interior, a small lobby off of which offices, a conference room, and the director's larger office are arranged. Beyond this suite stands a small kitchen that doubles as a smoking room. (No approved smoking areas yet; that would come later.) Floor-to-ceiling windows, part of the unreconstructed library building, look out on a central Moscow street. But although it dates from the 1970s, the Library for Foreign Literature doesn't look or feel like a Soviet building. Inside, everything is modern and bright, with blonde wood and new fixtures. The style, the color, the shape and texture of the furnishings feel emphatically un-Soviet.

Tania Feoktistova, the brilliant designer who heads the exhibition department at the Library for Foreign Literature, showed me potential exhibition spaces in the library, and together with Katia we chose one. We would hold the exhibition and our roundtable in the library's most elegant space, a lovely eighteenth-century building across the street. Before 1917, it was the house of a wealthy merchant. Katia and I walked over to see the space. We climbed the well-worn wooden stairs to a large open area, perfect for the exhibition, with a door into the Oval'nyi zal (Oval Hall), a splendid room with walls covered by floor-to-ceiling bookcases filled with old German books, their bindings visible through glass doors. What are these books?

I asked Katia, assuming they were part of the library's collection, perhaps some rare German books. This is the Library for Foreign Literature, after all.

Katia's answer startled me: they were German trophy books, confiscated from German libraries by the Soviet army in the last months of World War II. I was aware of such trophies, and I knew that Katia was deeply involved in a joint Russian-German effort to bring them out of cellars, warehouses, and libraries all over the former Soviet Union and countries of Eastern Europe, where they had been stashed since the end of the war. Some are immensely valuable; the Gutenberg Bible is hidden away somewhere in the Leninka. But I hadn't expected to see trophy books in the Library for Foreign Literature, although I should have. German books in the Library for Foreign Literature: why not? Katia and her staff had prepared careful lists and were prepared to return the books to their owners in Germany, if that ever became possible. If not, which seems likely—the Russian government is not eager to give back spoils of war such as priceless works of art—then at least Katia and her German counterparts are making the books accessible.

In the elegant surroundings of the Library for Foreign Literature we will sit for two days, an international group of scholars, artists, and other intellectuals, and converse about imperial and Soviet censorship surrounded by confiscated German books. Once again, Russia and Germany have been brought together uncannily. I am acutely aware of these books; they're almost a living presence. No wonder Katia is so involved with them! She tells me that she brought her German partner in the German-Russian trophy books project to the regional library in Smolensk, a city of fierce World War II battles, where they viewed a book exhibit. One of the books lay open in the case, and her German colleague looked at it intently. "This book came from my library," he observed. "See the stamp on the inside of the cover?" In a spontaneous gesture, the Smolensk librarian unlocked the case, took out the book, and handed it to him. "Take it home," she said. They were all silent for a moment. Of course, he couldn't take it home, and they all knew it; officials at the highest levels of government would become apoplectic. But if it were up to those librarians, the matter would have been resolved simply and directly among colleagues.

I discussed the concept of the exhibition and the catalog we would prepare with Viktor Moskvin, who was planning to curate the exhibition with me. (He later dropped out of the project and was replaced by Tania Feoktistova.) Inna Baldina, former head of the Leninka's *spetskhran*, came over from the Leninka and told me about her former job. I tried to imagine being the librarian in charge of the largest *spetskhran* in the world. I also met Sergei Mironenko, director of the State Archives of the Russian Federation, and Tania Goriaeva, one of Mironenko's staff members who had been conducting research on Soviet censorship that she was now able to publish. They greeted me warmly and promised to work with us on the exhibition. I found the same enthusiasm in every institution we approached: the Russian State Historical Library, the Russian National Library in St. Petersburg, and others.

GARDEN OF BROKEN STATUES TOUR, STOP 6: CENSORSHIP EXHIBITION IN MOSCOW

And what treasures we laid out, gathered from those archives and libraries! Imperial statutes and Soviet decrees. The catalog on which I had based my dissertation, and others like it, covering different ranges of years. Books from several foreign countries that had been banned throughout the Russian Empire. My examples from Illinois—the Brockhaus Encyclopedia *volumes and the world history—lay in a case next to other examples from Russian libraries. What would Professor Littman and his father think about those Odessa books coming back to Russia, even just for a month? We included dozens of books issued by Progress, a major Soviet publisher of popular works, but those exhibited were published in a secret series "for special use" with matching covers: Russian translations of foreign books deemed critical of the Soviet Union but useful for high-ranking party officials, such as memoirs by Konrad Adenauer and Henry Kissinger, books by or about Jimmy Carter, Fidel Castro, and Richard Nixon. I think it's safe to say that no one in the former Soviet Union—except, of course, some Communist Party folks— had walked through such a garden before.*

While we were gathering materials for the exhibition—seven hundred items had been included in the catalog—we were also gathering people to participate in the three-day roundtable that would take place after the opening. This wouldn't be the first time scholars had come together in Russia to discuss Soviet censorship; that honor went to colleagues in Leningrad, who held a conference in September 1991, just a month after the failed coup, while the Soviet Union still existed. We talked to the Leningrad organizers and agreed to publish their papers along with ours. But ours would be the first such meeting in post-Soviet Russia and the first with foreign as well as Russian participants.

Soon scholars inside Russia would be able to consult two published sources on Soviet censorship that many of them had never seen, volumes that came out of two émigré conferences held in the West during Soviet times. The first of these conferences took place in the United Kingdom in 1967, when Anatoly Kuznetsov spoke so movingly about self-censorship. The proceedings had been published in an invaluable little book, *The Soviet Censorship*, always within my reach when I am working.[2]

Maurice Friedberg and I organized the second émigré conference, held at the Smithsonian Institution in Washington, DC, in 1983. Following the London model, we invited mostly émigrés to speak, and afterward we edited and published the proceedings as *The Red Pencil*.[3]

More materials were to follow, based on the exhibitions and gatherings the Library for Foreign Literature and partners, as well as other institutions, organized inside post-Soviet Russia. The library's publishing house, Rudomino Publishers (named for the library's founder), published both the May 1993 Moscow exhibition catalog and the proceedings of our roundtable. Over the next two years, regional libraries and universities in the cities where we held exhibitions and conferences after Moscow brought out publications as well: St. Petersburg in 1994 and Tyumen and Yekaterinburg in 1995. Now there is a small but significant body of literature on imperial Russian and Soviet censorship that continues to grow, based on archival research, memoirs, interviews, and other sources previously closed to scholars. In some cases historians knew the material quite well but weren't allowed to publish any of it.

Our Moscow exhibition opened on May 24, 1993. The ceremony took place at 4 p.m., but Moscow radio and television arrived earlier to tape

---

2   Dewhirst and Farrell, *Soviet Censorship*.

3   Marianna Tax Choldin and Maurice Friedberg, eds., *The Red Pencil: Artists, Scholars, and Censors in the USSR* (Boston: Unwin Hyman, 1989).

interviews with Katia, Tania, and me. I have no idea what I said, or in what language, but it was probably a Russian-English hybrid, and pictures of some of the exhibition cases showed up on the nightly news. Over the next few days I heard from friends and colleagues all over Russia: "Hey! We saw you on TV last night!"

The timing of our roundtable was good. A year and a half after the end of the Soviet Union, participants had had a chance to look into various archives, exchange words with one another, and, perhaps most important, reflect on the subject. But they weren't yet taking their new situation for granted—far from it. I recall one Russian participant's remarks: "We're still able to express our thoughts about the censorship we endured only through inarticulate howls of pain. It will be years before we're able to distance ourselves sufficiently from that nightmare to talk about this phenomenon objectively, as scholars" (translation my own).

For three days we sat in the library's beautiful Oval Hall, surrounded by German trophy books, and talked. Most of our roundtable participants were Russians, which pleased us immensely: we wanted to hear about censorship from those directly affected, and howls of pain were perfectly acceptable. Mr. Solodin, the censor I met at the Leninka conference in October 1991, had agreed to speak. How would his erstwhile victims respond to him, I wondered? Inna Baldina, head of the Leninka's *spetskhran*, the largest in the country, would speak as well, along with academics, journalists, translators, theater directors, law specialists, and religious figures.

We also had the participation of Maurice Friedberg and Dmitrii Bobyshev, a Russian poet from St. Petersburg who had emigrated to the United States. Bobyshev taught at the University of Illinois and had translated many of my talks into a strong and elegant Russian. A handful of American graduate students and librarians came as well. Herman Ermolaev, a professor of Russian literature at Princeton who wrote about literary censorship, was there, and Steven Richmond, a doctoral student at the University of Chicago who specialized on the censorship of Soviet theater, spoke. From France came the director of the YMCA Press, Nikita Struve. Based in Paris, the press published works by dozens of Russians who had emigrated after 1917. One Italian also took part: Mario Corti, a journalist who had worked for decades for Radio Liberty, one of the "foreign voices," as they were known.

Along with Voice of America, the BBC World Service, Deutsche Welle, Kol Yisroel, and others, Radio Liberty had beamed uncensored news and views into the Soviet Union throughout the Cold War. And, to my delight, Ray and Jean Mortenson, Walter's son and daughter-in-law, came from New York for the week's events. They and Harvey sat together and happily observed the opening session, even though they didn't know any Russian.

At the end of the roundtable I invited anyone interested to watch a video of the American film *Doctor Zhivago*, which had been banned in the Soviet Union. A small group gathered around the screen to see Omar Sharif and Julie Christie. Pasternak's novel had been banned earlier, of course, and the author forced to refuse the Nobel Prize he had been awarded in 1958. The prize was posthumously accepted thirty years later, during glasnost.

The events in Moscow and St. Petersburg were incredibly exciting, but it was only when we took our show on the road to cities in Siberia—Tyumen, Tobolsk, and Yekaterinburg, in the Ural Mountains (all formerly closed cities)—that I realized how fortunate I was to be part of this project. Tanya,

Maurice Friedberg and Marianna Tax Choldin in St. Petersburg during the censorship exhibition and conference. They are standing by the entrance to a regional office for freedom of the press (October 1993)

our Moscow curator, had come up with a series of large panels depicting the materials in the exhibition. Viewers could follow along as though they were looking at items in glass cases and on the walls the way they had been displayed in Moscow and St. Petersburg. The panels were attractive and evocative as well as easy to move and manage.

Meanwhile, in each city, local librarians, archivists, and researchers had combed their own collections and curated magnificent exhibitions of their own, which they mounted very effectively. Tyumen and Tobolsk were on the route taken by prisoners exiled to Siberia in tsarist times. Both cities were founded by Cossacks in the late sixteenth century as Russia was expanding

Display case in Yekaterinburg exhibition

into Siberia; Tobolsk was for a time the capital of Siberia. Yekaterinburg, on the border of Europe and Asia, is an eighteenth-century city, perhaps best known these days as the place where the last tsar, Nicholas II, and his family were taken after the Bolshevik revolution and executed.

All three cities have natural beauty—great rivers, rolling hills, forests, some remnants of old wooden architecture—and colorful histories. But what I remember chiefly are the colleagues who collaborated with us to curate remarkable local exhibitions and who, by their own testimony, were moved deeply and changed by the experience. One Yekaterinburg librarian told me that she hadn't really thought much about censorship—she just took it for granted—until she got involved in archival research to prepare the exhibition, which is when she realized the extent of what had been done and how damaged they all had been by what I called omnicensorship.

Of the hundreds of experiences I've had on the road in post-Soviet Russia over the past twenty-plus years, I close this chapter with accounts of two. The first irritates me to this day; the second confirms for me that Katia and I have done some good and lasting work.

About fifteen years ago I was in the main public library in the southern Russian city of Rostov-on-Don, which neighbors the war zone of Chechnya. It's a multicultural area, and many civic groups there are concerned about tolerance. One such group had been working with children and had mounted an exhibition in the library of these children's drawings illustrating many of the articles of the UN Declaration of Human Rights.[4] It was a lovely exhibition that I was enjoying very much until I realized that Article 19, the right to free expression, was missing. Article 19 states: "Everyone has the right to freedom of opinion and expression; this right includes freedom to hold opinions without interference and to seek, receive and impart information and ideas through any media and regardless of frontiers." When I asked the director of the organization why Article 19 was not represented, she told me it was too abstract and complicated for the children to understand. I mentioned this later to a Russian colleague, a prominent human rights activist, who agreed that the concept was beyond little children.

---

4   Universal Declaration of Human Rights, adopted by the United Nations General Assembly on December 10, 1948.

But I disagreed vehemently. I knew well that even the smallest children were capable of understanding and exercising their right to free expression. They needed someone older to explain things, but that is, after all, what parents and teachers do. We mustn't underestimate children, and we mustn't deprive them of their human rights. I thought about myself as a small child, how I knew intrinsically that stifling expression was wrong and didn't hesitate to talk about it. I recalled a morning when I was in first or second grade. Our school librarian had asked me to be a student speaker on a panel addressing a conference of librarians in Mandel Hall, a large auditorium on the University of Chicago campus. I don't remember exactly what my topic was, but I do know that I told my audience forcefully that children should be able to read whatever they wanted. That day in Rostov-on-Don I vowed that I would tell this story whenever I could and do my best to persuade others to take children seriously.

In 2006 Katya and I collaborated with the Chicago Public Library on their ongoing "One Book, One Chicago" program. This time, however, two cities participated in the program—Chicago and Moscow—and promotional activities took place in both cities. The book we selected was Alexander Solzhenitsyn's gem *One Day in the Life of Ivan Denisovich*, which had been published in a prominent Soviet literary magazine in 1962, near the end of the Decade of Euphoria, and was the first account of gulag life to reach a wide audience.

Our Chicago week of programs included an introduction by Katia; an exhibition of gulag photos sent from Russia and displayed in the main building of the Chicago Public Library; two dramatic readings from *One Day in the Life*, a video conversation about the book between teenagers in both cities; and discussions in high-school and college English classes and public library book clubs. It was evident that Chicago readers didn't need to know a lot about Russia to understand Solzhenitsyn's message; they identified readily with Ivan Denisovich, the prisoner who lived his cold, hungry life with dignity.

Not surprisingly, Muscovites responded to *Ivan Denisovich* in deeply personal ways, and it's hard to find a Soviet family untouched by the gulag. Here are a few of my memories.

GARDEN OF BROKEN STATUES TOUR, STOP 7: GULAG

Nearly 350 people, youngsters as well as survivors, packed the library's large auditorium to see a French documentary on the gulag. We had planned to show half of the film—two and a half hours—but the crowd begged to see the whole thing. At a discussion in the American Center a man told us that he'd read One Day *when it first came out; he was thirteen. His taste ran to fantasy and adventure, but when he read this book, he was astonished and horrified to realize that he was reading about another world, a parallel world, but right here at home. The gulag was all around him. He has never forgotten the book or that sensation.*

Aleksandr Filippenko, a much-loved actor, performed a dramatic reading of the entire book against a backdrop of an enormous map of the Soviet Union dotted thickly with gulag sites (based on Solzhenitsyn's research). The audience, mesmerized, sat for hours.

We heard a piano concert of music written in the gulag by the composer Vsevolod Zaderatskii, who died shortly before Stalin's death, never gaining release. His son, a professor at the Moscow Conservatory, said his father composed while sitting on a log and had survived some of the worst places in the gulag for as long as he did because he was a terrific storyteller.

A dignified old man, a survivor of twenty-three years in the gulag in Norilsk, the world's northernmost city and home to nickel mines operated with slave labor, stood in front of Solzhenitsyn's map and presented to the library a three-volume set of Norilsk survivors' memoirs. He had been sent to Norilsk as an "American spy" because the Red Army found him in Frankfurt at the end of the war with American troops. Alas, this was a common story; the fictitious Ivan Denisovich was arrested as an American spy too. And America was not the only suspicious country; in the French film we saw about the gulag, an Esperanto speaker was arrested and sent to the camps because, according to the authorities, there's no country called Esperanto.

When I came to Moscow for the "One Book, Two Cities" events, my suitcase was full of materials from our Chicago program that I was bringing to present to Solzhenitsyn's wife. When I arrived at the airport, something highly unusual happened: there was a security check, and incoming passengers had to open their suitcases and go through them with an inspector. My Soviet censor stirred—at last the authorities would see what Marianna had been up to!—and I felt agitated as I prepared to show the inspector what I had. He examined my English-language books and guides for readers but paid special attention to a copy of *One Day in the Life of Ivan Denisovich* in Russian.

"So you like Solzhenitsyn?" he asked me, in Russian.

"Yes," I replied, also in Russian, "especially this book. We've just had a program about it in Chicago, and we're having a program here too, at the Library for Foreign Literature. I'm bringing this material to Solzhenitsyn's wife. The author himself is too ill to come."

"Oh," he said and asked me to tell him about the events. Feeling rather giddy, I mentioned the French documentary, the Filippenko dramatic reading, the concert, and the rest. He looked intently at me, then shook my hand.

"You are doing God's work," he said quietly. "Thank you."

CHAPTER 11

THE GARDEN OF BROKEN STATUES

I found my metaphor in 1997, although it took me some years to recognize it. For a long time I had been been trying to understand why I feel a visceral connection between censorship and memorials. My introduction to the Garden of Broken Statues turned out to be the key. Looking back, I could now ask the right questions, the ones that led me to an answer that satisfied me.

On that gloomy November day in 1997, I wondered whether I was in an outdoor museum or whether this strange park was perhaps a dump, a junkyard, for Communist symbols unwanted or embarrassing to the new Russian leadership. It was clear to me, as a student of Russian and Soviet history, that these works of crumbling stone and rusting metal were powerful symbols of the Soviet past loaded with significance for the generations familiar with that past, people who speak and understand Russian and its twentieth-century Soviet dialect.

Soviet is much more than a dialect, however; it's a point of view, a culture, and a way of life that lasted for seventy years. I've met men named Vladlen, a combination of the first syllables of the founder's name (Vladimir and Lenin). In the Palace of Weddings in Leningrad, now St. Petersburg again, as it was before the Bolshevik revolution, marble stairs were carpeted in worn red velvet, brides stood in long white dresses and veils and grooms in tuxedos, while a scratchy recording of the wedding march from *Lohengrin* played over and over—everything I expected at weddings that looked like that, except a Soviet official was presiding instead of a priest. In Soviet, God was bourgeois, opium for the masses, and not welcome in the Soviet Union. I haven't met a Vladlen lately; I've seen weddings with all the trimmings held in Orthodox churches and presided over by priests; and the Soviet joke appears to be dead, although it may be coming back under President Putin. Maybe the post-Soviet government would prefer if the past were forgotten, buried in the sands, like the ruins of the statue of Ozymandias, that ancient ruler of whom Shelley wrote so evocatively.

But if the Garden of Broken Statues was a museum and not a dump, I worried about future generations of visitors, starting with this immediate post-Soviet generation, a diminishing number of whom speak Soviet. I wondered what visitors from other countries would make of it as well. They'll have come to Moscow to see the sights and possibly stumble upon this one in their guidebook. The tourists won't understand much, I'm afraid. A few of the statues have plaques next to them, but they don't tell me much, and they'll tell innocent visitors even less.

The effect of this outdoor museum—if that's what it was—was disorienting, eerie, and rather shocking. What had these individuals done to earn statues in their honor? When had the statues been erected, by whom, and where had they stood? What should visitors know about the people and events they commemorate? Although I know both Russian and Soviet, I am bewildered. What about those visitors who know neither language? An interested visitor could probably read something about the garden and its statues on the Internet, but that would be an extra step. I like museums where I can learn about the place and its significance right there on site.

I didn't get back to the Garden of Broken Statues for sixteen years, although I'd been close to it a number of times while visiting the Tretyakov collections. But throughout the years I found myself thinking of the garden often, especially when I visited other sites in Russia or elsewhere that reminded me of it. And the questions connected with "speaking Soviet" continued to buzz gently in my head.

GARDEN OF BROKEN STATUES TOUR, STOP 8: SAKHAROV MUSEUM

That same November day in 1997 I visited the Sakharov Museum, named after the late Soviet physicist and human rights activist Andrei Sakharov.

Here I found, to my immense satisfaction, exhibits designed to teach people to understand Soviet. In the museum's first room were filmy panels with semitransparent images on them depicting symbols of an ideal socialism: throngs of sturdy laborers with outstretched arms bearing tools, images of power, strong yet graceful images of power. Across the aisle was a very different display: typed letters and documents, photographs, maps, official orders and directives, all portraying socialism as it really was in Stalin's Soviet Union.

The next room was shocking, a vast, dark warehouse fitted from floor to ceiling with narrow shelves and file drawers. Here and there, affixed to the drawers, were alphabetical lists of people executed in various parts of the gulag spread over this entire, vast country. The drawers contained as much information as could be gathered about individuals. Small photos of victims dotted the shelves. A few genuine items from the camps hung among the photos: a wooden cell window, a prisoner's striped uniform, a pickax used in the mines.

The Sakharov Museum impressed me as a model for how to portray the parts of a country's history that many of its citizens would prefer to forget. I had already visited another model, the headquarters of Memorial, an organization dedicated to searching out the truth about Soviet repression and documenting the fate of its victims to the extent possible.[1] Through Katia I'd met several of Memorial's leaders, and I admired them and their work enormously. I'd stood by the simple monument placed by Memorial on Lubyanka Square: a white stone from the remote northern Solovetskii Islands, home to Solovki Monastery, used in part as a prison in imperial times and the first camp in the Soviet gulag. I began to look for similar examples in countries I visited—displays prepared by libraries, archives, or museums.

Needless to say, my quest took me to the darkest places whose images haunted me at night. But I sought them out, perhaps obsessively, because I wanted to learn what people in various countries were being told about bad times in their own histories. A final troubling stop on my garden tour was as dark as they come, its complexities still unresolved.

---

1 Memorial's website is http://memo.ru.

GARDEN OF BROKEN STATUES TOUR, STOP 9: KATYN

I was in the Katyn Forest, near Smolensk, Russia, on a sunny day in January 2002. Katyn is a place where the earth is soaked with blood and the birds don't sing, or if they do, I was aware only of its deep silence. The snow was high and pure white, the air completely still, and my colleague and I were the only visitors that morning to the site of the massacre of more than 4,200 Polish military officers in the spring of 1940. For decades the Soviets had claimed that the Germans committed the massacre, and it was only after the Soviet Union collapsed that the truth came out.

A joint Polish-Russian memorial park was still under construction when I visited. The Poles had identified many of the executed individuals and built a reddish winding wall the height of a person with the names and information carved into the building blocks. As I wandered along the wall, I realized, with a sickening shudder, that once again the path on which I was walking was directly on top of a mass grave.

Eight years after my visit to Katyn, Polish blood flowed there again. To mark the seventieth anniversary of the massacre, a group of ninety-six Polish citizens, including surviving family members of the victims, the president, former president, and other political and military officials, flew to Smolensk. Despite dense fog, their Polish pilot, flying a Soviet-built Polish air force plane, attempted to land. No one survived the crash. In Poland, conspiracy theories continue to abound, all blaming the Russians for this disaster.

Since that November afternoon in 1997 in the Garden of Broken Statues, I found myself looking at monuments with new eyes. What did these statues reveal about the past? Was their tremendously powerful aura linked to attempts to explain the past objectively, or was it serving the needs of a particular group? It wasn't always easy to tell.

In late December 2013, during my fifty-third trip to Russia, I finally returned to the Garden of Broken Statues near the new building of the Tretyakov Gallery. It was as dreary a day as it had been when I first visited, and I was nearing the end of my book.

I am not the only person to have written about this garden. In the weeks after my trip, I read two descriptions, both by brilliant Russian émigrés. The late Svetlana Boym, a professor of Slavic and comparative literatures at

Harvard, published a book in 2001 called *The Future of Nostalgia*; chapter 8 includes a section called "Totalitarian Sculpture Garden: History as a Pastoral."[2] Boym had known about the Arts Park, as it was called then, from its beginning, when the Soviet Union ended on the last day of 1991 and sculptures began appearing there, deposited and desecrated by man and beast with cheerful abandon. By the time Boym went back to the park—the same year I visited, in 1997—she reported that some order had been imposed. A few statues were standing upright now, some back on their pedestals, and a small number had explanatory signs next to them.

"Statue Symbols," by Masha Gessen, was published in *The New York Times* while I was in Russia, a few days before my second visit to the park. The author is a journalist and writer born and raised in Moscow who emigrated to the United States twice, first with her family when she was fourteen. She then returned to post-Soviet Moscow to live and work, and re-emigrated to the United States in late 2013. Gessen had also seen the garden when it was new and when passion for change was strong and fresh. She traces its history from its beginnings as a disorganized dumping ground for statues of Soviet heroes to what it is now: a Soviet-style "official outdoor museum of sculpture."[3]

I confess that when I first read these pieces, I was intimidated. Strange, perhaps, after all my time in Russia, all my research, all the insight I've gained through the years. I chide myself: I should have more self-confidence. But Russia has that effect on me; I never know when I'll turn a corner and be jolted by unexpected emotions. This time I felt uncertain and humble. After all, both authors are native speakers of that Russian dialect I call Soviet; they know so much more than I do. What can I add to their wise and witty analyses, their ironic insights? But then I reconsidered. Of course, those statues call out to Svetlana Boym and Masha Gessen, whose first language is Soviet, as they must call out to Katia and all my intellectual friends in Russia. But they also call out to me, whose first language is English. I struggle continually to learn Soviet—not to speak it but to read and comprehend it.

---

2   Svetlana Boym, "Totalitarian Sculpture Garden: History as a Pastoral," in *The Future of Nostalgia* (New York: Basic Books, 2001), 192–226 (e-book).

3   Masha Gessen, "Statue Symbols," *The New York Times*, December 9, 2013 (online edition).

I'm compelled to write about Soviet, just as Masha and Svetlana, and probably countless others in Russia, are doing. And what I take away from my struggles is uniquely mine: it has to do with my life, my experience of Russia—through my family story, my fascination with censorship as a universal phenomenon, my studies, my ambivalence about the place.

Lena, a tall, beautiful woman in her early twenties from the international department of the Library for Foreign Literature, accompanied me on my 2013 visit to the garden. Lena was new to the library since my last visit, and I saw right away that she would fit into the International Department very well. Serious and committed to her job, Lena was a French major at Moscow State University working hard on her English. She seemed a little hesitant, maybe a little frightened of us, but I knew that wouldn't last long. Harvey was just the person with whom to practice English, and he'd put her at ease.

As we embarked on our visit, I realized that Lena was also just the right person to accompany me to this garden. Born in 1989, she grew up in post-Soviet Russia, living with her parents in the Stalin skyscraper across the street from the library, one of the seven famous "wedding cake" monuments that dot central Moscow. She was attuned to the many Soviet-era ghosts that inhabited her building, a monumental sculpture itself, with a frightening Soviet history. Her parents were both athletes—her father won a silver medal in crew in the 1988 Olympics—and they made sure that she knew their prestigious building's history.

After our time in the garden Lena took us on a tour of her building.

GARDEN OF BROKEN STATUES TOUR, STOP 10: STALIN'S SKYSCRAPER

We began in the garage, ordinary enough today but a source of fear for the child Lena, who knew from her parents that in Stalin's time it was home to a fleet of black Volga limousines that went out each night to collect people from their homes and deliver them to their doom. She pointed out the small kiosk in the building's main outdoor parking lot where, to this day, Dzerzhinsky's grandson, now an old man, spends time; for many years he was in charge of parking.

I had no doubt that once this twenty-four-year-old, raised amidst the ghosts of Dzerzhinsky's fleet of black Volgas, understood why I was interested

The garage from which Dzerzhinsky's fleet went out at night

in the sculptures, she would join in enthusiastically—and she did. Lena became my photographer, and we set off to see what we could see.

GARDEN OF BROKEN STATUES TOUR, STOP 11: THE GARDEN REVISITED

It was freezing cold and damp, a not-so-gentle wind was blowing, and the park was an icy, muddy construction zone. I don't know whether some new structure was being built or whether the authorities—which ones?— were improving the garden. I was eager to see the changes I'd read about: labels for some of the statues, selected figures returned to their pedestals, and other statues brought in to join the ones I saw sixteen years ago. Lena and I slipped and slid around the park, iPhones clutched in our cold hands. Construction workers and a grandfather pushing a stroller glanced at us quizzically. Tourists, even on a day like this! What's to see here? Their indifference was almost palpable, and I was glad; I wanted us to be invisible. My heart was beating fast as I stumbled along bumpy paths, Lena's hand protectively on my arm.

As we approached a brown sign near one of the statues, I saw at the bottom right the word "Muzeon," an unfamiliar term that Lena had been using. Wikidictionary tells me that "Muzeon" is an Esperanto noun, the accusative singular of muzeo, muzei in Russian, "museum" in English. What is the significance of using a word in Esperanto, an artificial language with close ties to Russia?

The sign near Dzerzhinsky's statue is in Russian and English: Dzerzhinsky, Felix Edmundovich (1877–1926). Included are the sculptor's name and dates, when and where the statue was cast in bronze (Leningrad, 1936), when it was erected in Moscow's Lubyanka Square (1958), when it was dismantled and moved to Muzeon (October 24, 1991). We read that "the work is historically and culturally significant, being the memorial construction of the Soviet era, on the themes of politics and ideology." The final sentence reads: "Protected by the state." At the bottom left, in large caps, is the word "Muzeon."

I found this text bewildering and deeply unsatisfying. While we learned all the fairly straightforward information about the statue and that the work is significant because it is a Soviet memorial having to do with politics and ideology, we weren't told who Dzerzhinsky was, why he had been deemed worthy of a monument, or what his connection to politics and ideology was. Shouldn't the viewer be told that Dzerzhinsky was the founder of the secret police; that Lubyanka Square is the site of the KGB headquarters, one of the most dreaded addresses in the Soviet Union, where who knows how many Soviet citizens were tortured and executed under Stalin? Boym puts it so gracefully:

> *If an extraterrestrial or any other not-so-well-informed stranger landed in Moscow and took a leisurely walk in the park, he would have had the impression that he is in a stable country that values its historical heritage and has had little experience with upheavals or revolutions. What is erased between the cautious lines of the sign is the history of the coup of August 1991 and people's unauthorized assault of the statue.*

I would add to that: also missing is the role of the secret police from its founding until the fall of the Soviet Union.

Gessen uses the Dzerzhinsky statue and those of other Soviet heroes to guide us from the events of August 1991 to the present. She writes:

> sometime in the 1990s fences appeared around the exiled monuments, turning the back lot into an official outdoor museum of sculpture. And then trucks came hauling all sorts of non-political sculptures, of anonymous people and assorted flora. The old Bolsheviks, being giant, did not exactly get lost among their new generic-looking neighbors; they just looked like monstrous plants in a fort of white plaster. . . . They certainly did not seem disgraced, or even deposed. The paint came off Dzerzhinsky and a placard went up on the fence. . . . The statue was no longer an exhibit; once again it was a monument.

I like this distinction: a good *exhibit* brings items together and explains their meaning, in historical context. A *monument* honors a particular person or event, in this case with no explanation of why the person or event is or was important. Dzerzhinsky, Lenin, Stalin, and others are simply present, with no connection made between them and the horrendous acts for which they were responsible. I saw only one label that did identify objects as museum exhibits, but it refers to a post-Soviet art installation in memory of gulag victims, donated by the sculptor Evgenii Chubarov to the city of Moscow and placed in the garden in 1998. The "old Bolsheviks," as Gessen calls them, stand nearby in heroic poses, tall on their pedestals. The tourist passing by might be forgiven for making no connection between them and Chubarov's disembodied heads packed neatly into wire and stone cages.

Our world is full of broken sculpture gardens; every country has some. Unlike the brilliant museums I described earlier, the ones that tell their brutal stories honestly, these unfinished gardens pulse not only with horror and sorrow but also with urgency, with the need to take down barriers, to see the past and the present with clarity, to show connections. They make me understand how very important it is for open democratic societies to give their citizens and the world's citizens access to *all* of the country's past, the shameful as well as the noble.

In countries that are not free, the rulers control the imagery and attempt to manipulate symbols to tell the story their way, forbidding or discouraging alternative versions. Opening access is an ongoing struggle even in democracies, including the United States of America. But at least in America we can talk, read, and write critically and publicly about black spots in our country's past and present. In countries where the state has a stranglehold on the press, where there is no freedom of expression, where the government's interpretation of history is the only acceptable and accessible one, dealing with those black spots, the ones "covered over with caviar," is a major challenge at best and life threatening at worst.

How is Russia going to manage? I find myself looking back at the 1990s with nostalgia, despite the scandals, many of them involving Big Money, that revealed some of what was going on behind the scenes—or out in the open—in the past few years. Many of us, including me, didn't pay enough attention. Despite those scandals, though, this is the decade upon which scholars of my generation, along with many of our Russian friends and colleagues, look back and weep with joy because we have lived long enough to experience it. I visited Russia two to four times each year during the 1990s, and every trip revealed to me a new country. Even though I know it was far from paradise, I still look back on those years as the Golden Age of post-Soviet Russia.

In my mind I revisit the KGB conference Katia and I attended on the way to the airport in the early 1990s. Thinking back on that scene, I realize that I should have been reluctant to dismiss so lightly what I had experienced there. The KGB was no joke. Something as powerful, sinister, evil, and deeply entrenched in society as the KGB doesn't just slink out quietly and fade away, never to be seen again. The KGB was and remains a rich, powerful, confident institution that flexes its muscles and takes charge. And once again, the KGB is alive and well in post-Soviet Russia.

Boris Yeltsin, the first president of post-Soviet Russia, appointed Vladimir Putin to be his prime minister in 1999. In 2000, Putin was elected president of Russia and served until 2008, when he switched places with his prime minister, Dmitrii Medvedev. They switched back in 2012, and Putin is now president again. For how long? No one knows.

Soon after Putin was elected president the first time, one of my closest Russian friends sat me down at the kitchen table, site of many serious political discussions in Soviet times, and pointed out to me how many newly appointed or elected officials had KGB connections. The list was a long one.

"That's how it will be," my friend said earnestly. "Mark my words: we'll be ruled now by KGB guys. We won't have the Soviet Union again, but we won't have your kind of democracy either, and we certainly won't have a free press."

My friend was right, of course. In the course of the following fourteen years, the chaotic, often joyous openness of the 1990s has disappeared, step by step. One of the first things I noticed was the 2002 shutdown of an enormously popular TV show called *Kukly* (puppets or dolls) that satirized important people, mostly politicians, Putin included. Investigative reporters who pressed too hard during the Chechnya wars and about corruption among officials began to be brutally silenced. Organizations such as the Sakharov Museum and Memorial that attempt to document the fate of gulag victims have been investigated and prosecuted. Opposition protesters and people with political ambitions have been jailed, some under horrendous conditions at former gulag sites. News programs on TV have reverted to the colorless, humorless, one-sided Soviet style so familiar to those of us who had to watch them in the past.

In the past year or two the government has passed several draconian (and absurd) laws: No "dirty words" in any kind of publication. No "propagandizing" for homosexuality. History books for schools, rewritten in the 1990s to replace Soviet distortions, are now rewritten again, with new distortions. The press and the Internet are being controlled in new ways. The liberal voice of the radio station Ekho Moskvy (Echo of Moscow) can still be heard, and some opposition papers and Internet sites are still being published, but for how long?

I thought I might lose my fear and discomfort after the Soviet Union collapsed, but I didn't. I suppose that I, the anthropologist's daughter, sense that cultures don't change so quickly, that there still may be cause for concern as I confront an unsmiling customs or immigration officer in a Russian airport. I realize now that borders in general, and Soviet and Russian borders in particular, are a powerful metaphor for me. They signify closed, controlled spaces where citizens lack basic rights.

I am an optimist and have been all my life. So here and there I find, somewhere in Russia, what I'll call Gardens of Openness, or, if not full-grown gardens, then at least patches where something good is growing. In Smolensk I saw Katyn Forest, but Katia made sure I also saw a Soros Foundation project that brought a big smile to my face. Smolensk had been full of military-related industries, a number of which were now being converted to civilian uses. I stood next to a large machine that looked like a coffeemaker, and a white-coated worker gave me a cup of fresh, warm, sweet soy milk to drink. My heart—and my vegetarian body—rejoiced. From machines of war and destruction, from Katyn, to the peaceful production of soy milk! How I want this little factory to survive!

The courtyard of the Library for Foreign Literature has become a new kind of garden—one of my Gardens of Openness—that began in 1994 with a bust of Heinrich Heine and continues blooming today with Erasmus, number 30, added in 2013. Each bust has its own story. In keeping with the library's mission and character, the busts come from many countries and represent many points of view. I list the countries here in alphabetical order: Azerbaijan, Belgium, Bulgaria, the Czech Republic, Egypt, Estonia,

Mary Choldin, Marianna Tax Choldin, Katia, Kate Choldin, and Iura with the bust of Machiavelli in the library's courtyard

The Abraham Lincoln bust in the courtyard of the library. Sculptor: John McClarey. The bust was a gift to the library from the Mortenson Center for International Library Programs, University of Illinois at Urbana-Champaign

Germany, Hungary, India, Iran, Ireland, Italy, Kyrgyzstan, Lithuania, Mexico, the Netherlands, Poland, Russia, Serbia, Slovenia, Sweden, the United Kingdom, the United States of America, and Venezuela.

James Joyce is here and Raoul Wallenberg, Father Aleksandr Men and Leonardo da Vinci, and Machiavelli.

I'm proud to be responsible for Abraham Lincoln's presence in the courtyard.

Whenever I'm in Moscow, I walk around and greet the busts. I'm always amused, and very touched, to see that visitors to the library—and they are mostly Russians—leave flowers by one or another bust, perhaps to mark a birthday or just out of respect.

I want so much for Russia to be a freer place, dotted with Gardens of Openness. My Russia-love remains strong, although mixed today with sadness, frustration, and disappointment. So much needs to be done; there are too many Gardens of Broken Statues in that vast territory. I've seen only a handful of them, some cared for but most still abandoned. I've wandered through these desolate gardens at all times of the year, but invariably I picture them in late fall or in winter, dark and cold, or perhaps with a pale sun and pure white snow, surrounded by impossibly tall, thin birch trees. The burden of cleaning up those gardens and caring for them, of turning them into open places, rests on my good Russian colleagues—but maybe I can help them a little. I plan to keep trying.

ACKNOWLEDGMENTS

In the winter of 2014 I came down with a bad case of pneumonia and had to be hospitalized. Tests showed that I had lung cancer. Harvey called Katia and gave her the bad news. A day or two later she called me to tell me that we really must be sisters, because she had just been diagnosed with kidney cancer and was going to Tel Aviv for treatment. A few excruciating weeks later, four days before surgery to remove half of my right lung, my doctors determined that I didn't have cancer after all; I merely had pneumonia cells that had gone crazy.

A few weeks after that revelation Harvey and I spent a week in Tel Aviv with Katia and Iura as she underwent one of many courses of chemotherapy; her cancer had metastasized. Despite the circumstances we had a lovely visit, chattering away as though nothing were wrong. Katia would come out of a grueling chemo session and head off to Jerusalem to give a lecture or plan a joint library project. After I returned home, I spoke with her nearly every day, in Tel Aviv, Moscow, London, Florence, Berlin, the Russian Far East, or wherever she happened to be. We rarely talked about her illness; she preferred to tell me what was going on in her library, conferences she was attending, and plans for publishing my book—this book—in Russia, in Russian, in 2016.

So I lived, and Katia, my sister-friend, died on July 9, 2015, after an intense and valiant battle. I owe her and her family, whom I love dearly, an enormous debt of gratitude. They took me into their lives, acknowledged my Russia-love with respect and sensitivity, forgave me my ignorance and often-fractured Russian, and interpreted for me a million things I didn't understand.

I am grateful to so many people in Russia, colleagues in Katia's library and all over the former Soviet Union. Special thanks to Galina Levina, who

Katia and Marianna in Tel Aviv (May 2014)

braved her dreaded English-language professor for my sake and allowed me to use her life stories in my book, and to my many friends on the staff of the Library for Foreign Literature for their gracious help.

June Pacha Farris worked with me for many years in the University of Illinois Library and now answers my calls for help in the University of Chicago Library. I'm most grateful to her and to my many friends in both these great libraries and universities. The Mortenson Center for International Library Programs at the University of Illinois, which I had the honor of creating and directing from 1991 to 2002, gave me the opportunity to meet and learn from hundreds of librarians from the former Soviet Union and countries all around the world, and I thank each one of them.

In 2014 and 2015 I lost two Urbana colleagues who were dear to me. Maurice Friedberg helped me immeasurably in the course of my censorship studies and kept me laughing while doing so. Ralph T. Fisher Jr., a wise and gentle man, directed the Russian and East European Center for much of my time there and supported me throughout my career. They would both be happy to see this book.

Over the past five years I've met frequently with a stalwart group of memoir writers—Carol Cade, Elizabeth Klein, Sena Leikvold, and Carol Poston—to each of whom I owe heartfelt thanks for generous reading and immensely helpful comments.

Thanks to Susan Dickman, who helped me tell my story; Devon Ritter, who got the manuscript in shape for publication; and Meghan Vicks, Kira Nemirovsky, Carolyn Pouncy, and others at Academic Studies Press, who have been generous with their help at the final stage of preparation.

Finally, thanks to my family. Harvey, my husband, is always my first reader and a great critic. Kate and Mary, my daughters, are unfailingly loyal and have been so patient each time I disappeared yet again into Russia. My four granddaughters—Jessie, Cooper, Jamie, and Teagan—will read this book when they're a little older and will, I hope, see their Nana and the world with new eyes.

Our family on Kate's and Mary's fiftieth birthday, April 18, 1965. From top left: Harvey, granddaughters Cooper and Jamie, Marianna, granddaughters Teagan and Jessie. Bottom: Kate and Mary

INDEX

CPSIA information can be obtained
at www.ICGtesting.com
Printed in the USA
FFOW02n0658080117
31014FF

9 781618 115447